I Woke Up One Day & Decided to LIVE!

A Biblical Study of Faith, Hope, & Victory

Carron Caldwell, MA, LPC-MITS

I Woke Up One Day and Decided to LIVE!
A Biblical Study of Faith, Hope, & Victory
Copyright © 2018 Carron Caldwell, MA, LPC-MITS

All Scripture quotations, unless otherwise indicated, are taken from the Holy Bible, King James Version.

All rights reserved. No part of this publication may be reproduced, stored in a retrieval system, or transmitted in any form or by any means – electronic, mechanical, photocopy, recording, or any other – except for brief quotations in printed reviews, without the prior permission of the publisher.

*Priority*ONE Publications
P. O. Box 361332 | Grosse Pointe, MI 48236
E-mail: info@priorityonebooks.com
URL: http://www.priorityonebooks.com

ISBN 13: 978-1-933972-59-6
ISBN 10: 1-933972-59-9

Editing by Patricia Hicks
Cover and Interior design by Christina Dixon

Printed in the United States of America

Contents

Foreword vii
Special Thanks... x
Acknowledgments xi
Introduction 13
Moses, A Prophet, Deliverer, and Lawgiver... 23
    Historical Leaders Raised Up By The Lord 30
    The Rev. Dr. Benjamin Elijah Mays words of counsel, wise wisdom, and a life-living perspective... 34
    Moral – Biblical and Life-Living 36
    Prayerful Reflection 37
Samson, A Judge of Israel... 39
    Man's Root of Temptation and Weakness for Women 42
    Moral – Biblical and Life-Living 57
    Prayerful Reflection 59
David, A Man After God's Own Heart.. 61
    Moral – Biblical and Life-living.. 71
    Prayerful Reflection 73
Incarcerated Prisoners, A Person that Allows Their Destiny to Unfold 75
    Biblical and Reality Presents Itself with Isolation............................... 83
    The Finale – Being A Prayer Warrior! 93
    Moral – Biblical and Life-Living 94
    Prayerful Reflection 96

Elijah, A Prophet of God in Contest With the Prophets of Baal 97
   Moral – Biblical and Life-Living 112
   Prayerful Reflection 117
A Samaritan Woman 119
   Moral – Biblical and Life-Living 127
   Prayerful Reflection 129
Blind Bartimaeus, A Man Who Cried Out for His Deliverance 131
   Moral – Biblical and Life-Living 135
   Prayerful Reflection 137
Life-Living Perspective 139
   Moral – Biblical and Life-Living 141
   Prayerful Reflection 142
Final Prayerful Reflection 143
References 145
About the Author 147

Foreword

Many struggles and difficulties in life revolve largely around mental health and addictions. *"I Woke Up One Day & Decided to Live"* is an eye-opening and mind-boggling experience to the soul to obtain faith, hope, and victory over mental health challenges, and a merciful God that gives His people grace, favor, and victory in midst of trials and tribulations. He is a "show up" God in the face of adversity and the snares of the enemy!

Mental health illnesses are real. It is amazing how Carron Caldwell articulates and parallels the effect of mental health difficulties to Bible leaders and prophets with everyday individuals. Being a pastor for four years, and a treatment/ specialized foster/adoptive parent for more than 35 years, has given me both experiences and struggles in the ministry. It has also allowed me to join collaboratively with licensed professionals in therapy, church members, family members, mental health treatment agencies, children, and individuals within the community. The Biblical passage of 1 Corinthians 15:46 elaborates on the natural and then spiritual, which helps one to understand that after deliverance has come, then one seeks the evidence of deliverance. My Sunday morning program states: "Program subject to change by the move of the Holy Ghost." This merely says: "When the spirit of God enters the room, be ready to throw the printed program away, and let God have His way!"

The same concept is exercised with the diverse mental health issues. Yes, the preacher may say: "you can rise above depression, anger, and many other addictions if you can just believe and trust in the miracle works of God." Matthew 9:29 states: "Then touched he their eyes, saying, According to your faith be it unto you." Therefore, those dealing with mental health, health issues, or whatever the circumstance should follow the doctor's instructions first. They should also continue the regiment of medical care, until your Godly faith kicks in and God gives you a complete medical breakthrough: "And he charged him to tell no man: but go, and shew thyself to the priest, and offer for thy cleansing, according as Moses commanded, for a testimony unto them" (Luke 5:14). The priest was responsible for verifying the evidence of their healing. The evidence today is to go back to your doctor for proof.

After a miracle of deliverance, continue with your doctor's instructions, until you visit your doctor to confirm the anomaly once seen in your body is no longer present. Afterward, when the X-rays, blood tests, and other tests are complete, and the doctor (as the priest) states that "you are no longer in need of his care," continue to give God the praise. At that time, throw the medicine away, and give God the praise and glory. For you are now healed and have obtained victory over your condition. As always, get the evidence of your deliverance.

This book sheds light to enhance one in knowing needed areas of mental health and addictions. This book also presents Biblical principles that are manifested in our churches and society as a whole. God is still working miracles, and He is the same yesterday and today. You are breathing, aren't you? It is also understood that people are not all on the same level of their belief. This includes many who claim to have much faith and did not receive deliverance for everything they believe God for. We are to never judge or criticize anyone's belief system: "JUDGE not, that ye be not judged" (Matthew 7:1). Luke, the beloved physician and disciple of Jesus Christ, preached faith in Jesus for healing and deliverance. At times, this man of God also functioned in his occupational profession, where he prescribed medicine to those in need.

Our Heavenly Father and Creator in His infinite wisdom knows the struggles of the human mind and body. He wants us to be happy, healthy, and holy. He understands the differences in individuals and belief systems. God has provided helps for all of us to survive. Help comes in the form of medical doctors, psychiatrists, psychologists, therapists, scientists, and the likes to find breakthroughs in medicines, lawyers, judges, and many other offices of helps to advocate for one's survival. 2 Peter 1:3 reflects on how the Creator has given people all things to survive: "According as his divine power hath given unto us all things that pertain unto life and godliness, through the knowledge of him that hath called us to glory and virtue."

I thank God for allowing such a knowledgeable, educated, and Christian woman as Carron Caldwell to influence my life in a positive and spiritual manner. She has been a powerful impact to my community and many communities throughout this country. I believe that as many as possible should advocate for more medical and financial resources in support of cures for mental health concerns, and to pursue Godly leaders to lead God's people and sinners into the House of God (see Titus 1:5-9).

Thank you, Carron Caldwell, for your inspiration to individuals, while working in the State of New Mexico, and at my church.

Elder James Walker, Pastor
Faith Tabernacle Church of God in Christ
Albuquerque, New Mexico

Special Thanks

Special thanks to Minister Christina Dixon from PriorityONE, who gave me a chance to publish my book, and who acknowledged me as a "Christian writer." Words can never say "thank you." You are a Godsend to me, and I believe others can testify the same.

Acknowledgments

To my Lord and Savior Jesus Christ, who hears and answers the prayers of the righteous: "The LORD is far from the wicked: but he heareth the prayer of the righteous" (Proverbs 15:29). Rev. Dr. Peggy Way (Nashville, TN), a doctoral professor at Argosy University, who gives a guiding hand to her students, as she reflects on the perils of life from a Biblical and practical life-living perspective. Elder James Walker (Albuquerque, NM), pastor of Faith Temple Church of God in Christ, a called pastor that exemplifies Jeremiah 3:15. Prior to moving across the country, I called several churches in the area for fellowship, and to no avail not one returned call. Pastor Walker, an exceptional pastor in the area, responded to me, and I shall always be grateful. Dr. Henry Dandridge (Detroit, MI), a clinical psychologist at Emmanuel House, who gave me an opportunity as an intern, when I looked far and beyond, and to no avail. The late Elder Louis Caldwell (Nashville, TN), former pastor of Gospel Tabernacle Church of God in Christ, my former father-in-law and my former pastor who taught me Biblical principles as a babe in Christ Jesus, and who introduced me to the knowledge of tithes: "Bring ye all the tithes into the storehouse, that there may be meat in mine house, and prove me now herewith, saith the LORD of hosts, if I will not open you the windows of heaven, and pour you out a blessing, that there shall not be room enough to receive it" (Malachi 3:10). RIP Pastor Louis Caldwell. Ernestine Williams (Nashville, TN), my aunt, who has the gift of giving. Elder Vincent E. Mathews, Sr. (Port Huron, MI), pastor of All Nations Church of God in Christ, who loves the Lord more than anything else. The late Barbara Hunter (Nashville, TN), my bestest friend for over thirty years, who introduced me to the world of academia. "I really miss us talking every day." RIP bestest friend. To the men, women, and youth offenders in

Michigan, Tennessee, and New Mexico behind prison walls, who helped me with the practical side of ministry and therapeutic interventions. A special acknowledgement to Waldell Fisher (gifts of ministry), Randall White (great sense of humor, a walking concordance, awesome gift as a keyboard player: "I hope I didn't move too many chairs around in changing things"), Dwight Wright (God's gift with a musical ear on any keyboard), Annette Elliott (a songbird), C. Smith (a for real - for real armourbearer), Michael 2X (can make some great Kool-Aid), Timothy Parham (never had a instrumental lesson, and can make any musical instrument talk), Steven Murphy "Red" (a person open to therapeutic counseling), and David Turner (the gift of language). These men, women, and youth exhibit great talents, gifts, and abilities that only God Himself has given. A shout out to my Zeta Phi Beta Sisters around the globe – "keep blue and white visible." The cherish years of life with my three adult children: Quanette, Louis II, and Angel. Last, but not least, my six siblings: "We shared common themes growing up, and as adults differences prevail."

Introduction

"MAN that is born of a woman is of few days, and full of trouble."
Job 14:1

"The thief cometh not, but for to steal, and to kill, and to destroy: I am come that they might have life, and that they might have it more abundantly."
John 10:10

The purpose of picking up the pen to write this Biblical study is twofold. The first aim is to put my Lord and Savior Jesus Christ on the map in a concise way. I so often hear some Believers say: "I don't understand the Bible." Therefore, many can see Biblical principles unfold and manifest themselves in today's society. The second aim entails being a part in building up the Kingdom of Jesus Christ. Some of the best-selling books under the umbrella of "Christianity" entail "drama in the church" – how leaders and others have entangled themselves in ungodly behavior(s), church folk's business, deep profanity, and how to make church business work for one's own good. Therefore, I reflect upon words my mother would periodically say to her children who got caught up in bad situations: "You'll just give people something to talk about." Well, some "church folks" have given some best-selling authors something to write about.

A part of this book title comes from a preached sermon I heard: "Wake Up and Live!" The pastor could not finish his sermon because many in the church went up with a "shout of praise." Therefore, I asked myself: "Did something hit home to cause them to wake up and live, and/or was it a Rhema (a right now word) word from on high?" Therefore, the saints of God can forever keep at the forefront: "Likewise the Spirit also helpeth our infirmities: for we know not what we should pray for as we ought: but the Spirit itself maketh intercession for us with groanings which cannot be uttered" (Romans 8:26); "Who is he that condemneth? It is Christ that died, yea rather, that is risen again, who is even at the right hand of God, who also maketh intercession for us" (verse 34).

The words saints, Believers, and Christians are used interchangeably to represent people who have given their lives to Jesus Christ. It is the author's prayer and hope that this book will be used to facilitate Bible studies, small group discussions, and in one's personal reading and studying.

It has been said that many people do not read the preface, foreword, or the introduction in books. They jump right into reading the first chapter. I must say: "I too, at times, follow this path." In reading the preface/foreword and introduction, it can be like peeling an orange. You must get past the peeling to get to the juice and nourishment inside.

It has been a joy along with some challenges in researching and writing this book. I have found myself reflecting on weekly Bible studies, my studies in Theology and Seminary schooling, life-living situations, testimonies of the saints, and reflecting on preached words as preachers would act out their sermons and incorporate the congregation as they gave their amen, hallelujah, thank you Jesus (a call and response), hand waves, colorful handkerchiefs waved in the air, and shout of praise. The preacher would say: "If you don't want to say amen, say ouch." At times, I would say to myself during the sermon: "ouch, ouch, ouch; Lord let me get it together." Some people testify they were raised in the church. This is not my

Introduction

testimony because I received salvation as an adult, and was a true novice to the Bible, church, church people, and the area of Christianity. Therefore, church people would have called me: "a babe in Christ." After accepting Christ, I fell in love with my Lord and Savior Jesus Christ and began to read and study the Bible. Later I became a prayer warrior (due to trials and tribulations). Have I missed the mark at times? Yes, and who hasn't? But because of my love for Jesus and quest for Biblical knowledge, I chose to launch out and to attend Theological and Seminary schooling. Upon graduating, I wanted to implement and work alongside others in Christian education ministry. But I was told: "You're not the only one that went to theology/seminary school." Therefore, I decided to use my theology knowledge as a "Christian writer," and to embrace those who have a love and concern for outreach ministry.

Ministry is very broad, and one must find their niche (calling) in ministry. Outreach ministry is my niche, as it continues to challenge and stretch me in ministry. Outreach ministry is so vibrant and needed, especially when I occasionally reflect on a young woman's testimony I heard over thirty plus years ago: "I tried different men, prostitution, illegal drugs, partying, and suicide attempts. I have even tried some churches and some church people, and the result entails being despondent with the hurdles in the church, and a saying from a pastor in his preaching regarding people": "I have found out that people are people - in the church and out the church." According to the Bible, there should be something different about the household of faith: "But ye are a chosen generation, a royal priesthood, an holy nation, a peculiar people; that ye should shew forth the praises of him who hath called you out of darkness into his marvellous light: Which in time past were not a people; but are now the people of God: which had not obtained mercy, but now have obtained mercy" (1 Peter 2:9, 10).

I Woke Up One Day & Decided to LIVE!

There has indeed been a paradigm shift in the Body of Christ, where some churches and ministries today, put more emphasis on the commercial (business) side, than on the spiritual realm (things of the Lord) in the Body of Christ. This paradigm shift has caused some former church members and people in general to slack up on going to church, and some have stopped going altogether. Some of them are going to live plays, musical concerts, listening to sermons on television, and having church at home without all the hurdles and emotional distress in the church. It appears that Satan and his angels are using God's own people (especially leaders) as participants in trying to destroy the church – the *Ecclesia*, and some church folks are joining with them. This demonstrates two sides of the same coin, where some leaders sway more on the commercial side, and some saints in the Body of Christ follow the leader. It reminds one of the childhood games – "Follow the Leader" and "Simon Says."

Therefore with sadness and grief, the end results lead to more dollar lines than prayer lines, buy a ticket to hear the preached word, join online membership (which offers very little or no rapport with church members), taking more time to swipe a credit card than praying for a distressed soul, leaders and others in sins of immorality, little to no repentance of one's sin, usher greets one with an offering envelope versus a church bulletin ("you can get that on our website"), and a host of ungodly things in the household of faith. Unfortunately, some churches and ministries are more about business than souls, and not too keen on building up the Body of Christ. It appears to be more about titles, positions, ungodly relationships, money... ! I really miss some parts of "old school teaching" in the church. The saints would pray for you and would not let you go until deliverance came. I believe at that time, the majority of the saints cared about people and ministry.

Introduction

The antidote (remedy, cure, answer) to this paradigm shift is to **uphold the mission of Jesus Christ**: "THE SPIRIT OF THE LORD IS UPON ME, BECAUSE HE HATH ANOINTED ME TO PREACH THE GOSPEL TO THE POOR; HE HATH SENT ME TO HEAL THE BROKENHEARTED, TO PREACH DELIVERANCE TO THE CAPTIVES, AND RECOVERING OF SIGHT TO THE BLIND, TO SET AT LIBERTY THEM THAT ARE BRUISED. TO PREACH THE ACCEPTABLE YEAR OF THE LORD" (Luke 4:18, 19); to **be a called pastor**: "And I will give you pastors according to mine heart, which shall feed you with knowledge and understanding" (Jeremiah 3:15); to **be a beaming light in ministry**: "Do ye not know that they which minister about holy things live of the things of the temple? and they which wait at the altar are partakers with the altar? Even so hath the Lord ordained that they which preach the gospel should live of the gospel" (1 Corinthians 9:13, 14); and to **embrace the love and care of Jesus Christ in humanity** (see John 4:4-29).

In the Bible and in life-living, there are trials and triumphs on every side. The Apostle Paul said it well that in the midst of trials: "We are troubled on every side, yet not distressed; we are perplexed, but not in despair; Persecuted, but not forsaken; cast down, but not destroyed" (2 Corinthians 4:8, 9). Oftentimes, the trials more than the triumphs cause a person to drop out of the race, to give up, and for some, unfortunately, to commit suicide. One of Aesop's Fables, *The Hare and the Tortoise*, was where the tortoise challenged the hare in a race. The hare thought it was a joke because he moved so fast and the tortoise was a slow mover. During the race, the hare got out of the race to have fun; the tortoise stayed in the race, his mind on making it to the finish line. The moral of this story: "The race is not always to the swift." The Pauline epistle states: "Know ye not that they which run in a race run all, but one receiveth the prize? So run, that ye may obtain" (1 Corinthians 9:24). The apostle ran so well, that near the end of his journey he used "I statements" (what psychotherapists periodically encourage their clients to use): "I have fought a good fight, I have finished my course, I have kept the faith" (2 Timothy 4:7). The Apostle Paul did not blame others for the trials and tribulations he endured.

Throughout the Bible we read about leaders, prophets, prophetesses, and others who **Decided to Wake Up and Live** after an encounter with the Lord. Some of them including many of us thought: "This is my niche," my comfort zone, my calling; then God spoke into their life and moved them into their destiny.

Elijah, a great prophet, received a death threat from Jezebel: "So let the gods do to me, and more also, if I make not thy life as the life of one of them by to morrow about this time" (1 Kings 19:2b). This caused the prophet to run until he was exhausted; then he sat under a juniper tree and said: "It is enough; now, O LORD, take away my life; for I am not better than my fathers" (verse 4b). The prophet Elijah did not die under the juniper tree because God came to him; he spoke God's word into the lives of Israel's leaders, until he was taken away by God in a chariot of fire.

Moses, a humble man, was chosen by God to lead the children of Israel out of Egypt. The Bible says that Moses was content in Midian, comfortable in his life as a shepherd: "And Moses was content to dwell with the man: and he gave Moses Zipporah his daughter" (Exodus 2:21). Moses was living on the backside of Midian, had gotten married, had children, and was a shepherd to his father-in-law, Jethro. God used this humble man to become a great spokesman for God and the deliverer of Israel.

The Samaritan woman, a mixed race, and an outcast had a spiritual encounter with Jesus that changed her community. Jesus went out of

Introduction

His way and made sure nobody was around to be critical, judgmental, nor biased to the Samaritan woman at Jacob's Well. Jesus took on the role as a psychotherapist, where he listened to her story, and He was an effective witness to the woman who was considered an outcast. This Biblical passage (John 4:4-30) of the Samaritan woman at Jacob's Well is a blueprint on how to be an effective witness. Oftentimes, some saints are so critical, biased, and judgmental when going down memory lane with someone's past, when they really should look at the beam in their own eyes: "Or how wilt thou say to thy brother, Let me pull out the mote out of thine eye; and, behold, a beam is in thine own eye? Thou hypocrite, first cast out the beam out of thine own eye; and then shalt thou see clearly to cast out the mote out of thy brother's eye" (Matthew 7: 4, 5). In being an effective witness, one must have compassion and not think they are a "better than thou person" (self-righteousness). One should always keep at the forefront: "If it wasn't for the grace of God, go I": "But by the grace of God I am what I am: and his grace which was bestowed upon me was not in vain; but I labored more abundantly than they all: yet not I, but the grace of God which was with me: (1 Corinthians 15:10).

Samson, a miracle child from a barren mother, had a secret that he could not share. A woman whom Samson loved caused him to reveal his secret. In revealing his secret, Samson fell into the hands of his enemies, the Philistines; who gouged out his eyes and put him into prison. The opportunity for redemption presented itself when the Philistines brought Samson out of prison to entertain them, when their hearts were merry (see Judges 16:25). Samson's heart had changed towards God and he took the opportunity to ask God: "And Samson called unto the LORD, and said, O Lord GOD, remember me, I pray thee, and strengthen me, I pray thee, only this once, O God, that I may be at once avenged of the Philistines for my two eyes" (verse 28).

I Woke Up One Day & Decided to LIVE!

We read and hear about countless deaths by suicide, attempted suicides, and about those in our family and loved ones affected by this tragedy. The late Rev. James Cleveland's song, *I Stood On the Banks of the Jordan*, speaks about how he saw his mother being taken away by death (not suicide). This song is similar to a young lady's testimony I once heard – "I stood on the banks of the river and walked to the edge of the banks and said, 'what's the use in living?' I just needed to take one more step and the current of the waters would have taken me under. But God, who is rich in mercy, loved me when I didn't love myself. In the midst of this suicidal attempt, something said, 'Go back.' I did an about face and thought no more about my life troubles nor suicide."

Two years later, the demon of depression showed up again, and I said: "I'm going to take a handful of pills, go to sleep, and not wake up." Again, God's mercy prevailed. She said in her testimony: "I was a person that knew of the Lord Jesus Christ, but did not have a personal relationship with Him." Twenty plus years passed and no suicidal thoughts emerged. It is without attesting that sometimes life just gives one a curveball. This sister mentioned in the trials of her life, she found herself going again to the medicine cabinet and looking at the pills. Afterward, she closed the medicine cabinet and sat down. As she sat there toiling over death and life, a "still small voice" from the Lord spoke to her: "If you could see your future." She was reminded of a preacher in his message who said: "Just to hear a word from the Lord will make everything alright. A person's situation may not change, but just knowing you heard the Lord's voice makes everything alright." The emotional hurdles took its toils on this young lady, but when she heard a Rhema word from the preacher, this young lady: **"Decided to Wake Up and Live!"**

While unfortunately, there are some with an addiction, a diagnosed or undiagnosed mental disorder or just some life-living situations

Introduction

when it felt all hope was lost who have sought refuge in suicide. On the other hand, there are those like the prophet Elijah, with a death wish, who had an encounter with God, whose life became more vibrant than ever.

This book will implement layers of Biblical, historical, theological, counseling, and life-living situations that add to one's faith and hope in being victorious in the face of adversity. It is with prayer that we too will see how in the midst of trials and tribulations, God steps into our situation for deliverance in His own way, and He guides one into their destiny: "GOD is our refuge and strength, a very present help in trouble" (Psalm 46:1). Therefore, it is without attesting to the gospel singer, (Dottie People's) song *"He's an On Time God."*

The grace of our Lord Jesus Christ be with you all. Amen (Revelation 22:21).

> In His Service,
> Carron Caldwell, MA, LPC-MITS

Moses, A Prophet, Deliverer, and Lawgiver

No Contentment, When I Hear the Cries of My People

"And the LORD said, I have surely seen the affliction of my people which are in Egypt, and have heard their cry by reason of their taskmasters; for I know their sorrows; And I am come down to deliver them out of the hand of the Egyptians, and to bring them up out of that land unto a good land and a large, unto a land flowing with milk and honey; unto the place of the Canaanites, and the Hittites, and the Amorites, and the Perizzites, and the Hivites, and the Jebusites."

Exodus 3:7, 8

The name Moses means "drawn out." This man's life is divided into 40's. Forty years he was in Pharaoh's house, forty years on the backside of Midian, and forty years in the wilderness with the children of Israel. He lived to be 120 years old, without losing his faculties: "And Moses was an hundred and twenty years old when he died: his eye was not dim, nor his natural force abated" (Deuteronomy 34:7). In the midst of Moses leading Israel, a rebellious nation, his natural body was not affected.

Moses, a fugitive in the land of Midian, had gotten married, had children and was a shepherd to his father-in-law Jethro. The Bible says: "And Moses was content to dwell with the man: and he gave Moses Zipporah his daughter" (Exodus 2:21). A threat from Pharaoh caused Moses to flee and live as a fugitive (in today's vernacular, Moses would be considered "absconded"). Therefore, the fugitive established a new life in his new-found community with his nuclear family, in-laws, and others.

When Moses was on Horeb, the mountain of God, something unusual happened which drew his attention. Moses saw a bush burning that would not be consumed: "And Moses said, I will now turn aside, and see this great sight, why the bush is not burnt" (Exodus 3:3). God saw that he had Moses' attention, calling his name twice. Moses responded: "Here am I" (verse 4b). Upon receiving a response from Moses, God gave him the historical fact that He is: "the God of thy father, the God of Abraham, the God of Isaac, and the God of Jacob" (verse 6a). This was a God call to leadership for Moses. God told Moses about his people and how he heard their cry, saw their tears, and knew their sorrows because of their taskmasters: "And the LORD said, I have surely seen the affliction of my people which are in Egypt, and have heard their cry by reason of their taskmasters; for I know their sorrows; And I am come down to deliver them out of the hand of the Egyptians, and to bring them up out of that land unto a good land and a large, unto a land flowing with milk and honey; unto the place of the Canaanites, and the Hittites, and the Amorites, and the Perizzites, and the Hivites, and the Jebusites" (verses 7, 8).

Moses had been away from his family of origin for forty years. One can imagine his sense of abandonment, periodically reminiscing about his family, his loved ones, and his people in general. Because of the threat of being slain by Pharaoh, Moses was a fugitive and could not go back home. But, because of Israel's cry, God called Moses to go back into Egypt to Pharaoh's house and speak His words of deliverance: "Come now therefore, and I will send thee unto Pharaoh, that thou mayest bring forth my people the children of Israel out of Egypt" (Exodus 3:10).

Moses, A Prophet, Deliverer and Lawgiver

Prior to the new Pharaoh, the children of Israel were not enslaved. But a new Pharaoh came on the throne: "And it came to pass in process of time, that the king of Egypt died: and the children of Israel sighed by reason of the bondage, and they cried, and their cry came up unto God by reason of the bondage" (Exodus 2:23, 24). In hearing the cries of His people, God called Moses into leadership to deliver His people out of bondage. God told him to go and promised that He would certainly be with him. But Moses did not welcome this calling.

Moses had a question for God: "If the people asked who sent him, what shall he say?" God responded with the name: "I AM." Moses continued to be hesitant about the call. He began to focus on the rejections of the people, of them not believing him: "But, behold, they will not believe me, nor hearken unto my voice: for they will say, The LORD hath not appeared unto thee" (Exodus 4:1b).

According to the Bible, Moses was content where he was in Midian; but there can be no contentment when the people of God are crying out for deliverance from bondage. God will raise up "a Moses" to come and deliver His people out of bondage. God saw their tears, He heard cries that came into His ears, and he saw taskmasters mistreating His people; therefore, He raised up Israel's "homeboy" to go into Egypt to Pharaoh's house and tell him: "Thus saith the Lord." In spite of all of Moses' reasons for not going into Egypt, asking God to send another, even inquiring who sent him, and his preoccupation with rejections from the people, God basically said to Moses: "No Moses, it is my people whom I made a covenant with, and I continually hear their cries of bondage."

Growing up as a child, when the children did not obey, my mom would say, "I'll show you better than I can tell you." God had to show Moses better than tell him: "And the LORD said furthermore unto him, Put now thine hand into thy bosom. And he put his hand into his bosom: and when he took it out, behold, his hand was leprous as snow" (Exodus 4:6). God used miracles of showing better than telling: "And he said, Put thine hand into thy bosom again. And he put his hand into his bosom again; and plucked it out of his bosom, and, behold, it was turned again as his other flesh" (verse 7). God was telling Moses, "No, No, No, I have heard the cries of My people which are in Egypt, I have seen their tears, and I know their sorrows. No contentment Moses; I have called their homeboy Moses to deliver my people out of the hand of bondage." Yes, Moses was their homeboy because he was an Israelite, with an upbringing as an Egyptian in Pharaoh's house. When Moses saw an Egyptian punishing a Hebrew, he killed the Egyptian guard and buried him in the sand. Later, he was asked: "Who made thee a prince and a judge over us?" (Exodus 2:14a) Afterward, he told Moses about his murder: "intendest thou to kill me, as thou killedst the Egyptian (verse 14b)? To keep from being slain by Pharaoh, Moses fled the scene and started a new life.

Moses continued to have reservations about his call as God's spokesman and deliverer to the children of Israel. This time, Moses clung to his shortcoming of having a speech problem: "I am not eloquent... I am slow of speech, and of a slow tongue" (Exodus 4:10b). God's response came back with a rhetorical question about His creation of man: "And the LORD said unto him, Who hath made man's mouth? or who maketh the dumb, or deaf, or the seeing, or the blind? have not I the LORD" (verse 11)? Moses still tried to detour from this assignment, wanting God to send someone else. This made God angry, because Moses was His choice to be the deliverer of His people, Israel. "No, God told Moses. I'm not sending someone else! I've chosen you, Moses, to go into Egypt to deliver my people Israel out of bondage!"

Moses, A Prophet, Deliverer and Lawgiver

In the book of Isaiah, another transition to Isaiah call was made, "Whom shall I send, and who will go for us" (Isaiah 6:8b)? The prophet Isaiah had gotten himself together and responded: "Then said I, Here am I; send me" (verse 8b). Moses' response was a mixture of still being content with his current life, passing the buck, feeling inadequate because of speech problems, and fear of rejections from the people. The underlying factor for Moses lay in his fear in going back and being killed. To soothe Moses's fear: "And the LORD said unto Moses in Midian, Go, return into Egypt: for all the men are dead which sought thy life" (Exodus 4:19). On the same note: "Was it Moses's fear of rejections from the people – his own people?"

When the Lord calls one into leadership, He will not let them go empty-handed. God reminded Moses about his brother, Aaron, who would be his mouthpiece: "And he shall be thy spokesman unto the people: and he shall be, even he shall be to thee instead of a mouth, and thou shalt be to him instead of God" (Exodus 4:16). In the end, God returned Moses into Egypt with a rod and said: "And thou shalt take this rod in thine hand, wherewith thou shalt do signs" (verse 17). When my last child left home, he was excited to join the adult world. His girlfriend came to help him pack his belongings. I sat in a chair as they walked back and forth, excited about been together, and away from their parent(s) house. After getting his last belongings, I gave my son words of counsel: "You be careful out there son, there are wolves out there, and if you're not careful, they'll eat you up." He looked at me with assurance saying: "Moma, I'm grown, and I have to be on my own!" Moses was grown and sought permission and wise counsel from an adult, his father-in-law, Jethro.

It is with a prideful self-reliance that some leaders called by God, will not seek permission, guidance, wise counsel, or blessings from their pastor or others in authority. They have been called by God,

I Woke Up One Day & Decided to LIVE!

licensed and ordained to do ministry, and will take themselves, briefcase, and even some members of the church to start a church without having a working alliance or rapport with the pastor or person of authority. Moses did not exemplify this behavior. The Bible states: "And Moses went and returned to Jethro his father in law, and said unto him, Let me go, I pray thee, and return unto my brethren which are in Egypt, and see whether they be yet alive" (Exodus 4:18a). His father-in-law gave his permission and guidance: "Go in peace" (verse 18b). On the same note, some men will do evangelist ministry and often leave their family at home, with the wife to carry the responsibilities of the family - when God has called the man as the head of the house: "For the husband is the head of the wife, even as Christ is the head of the church: and he is the saviour of the body" (Ephesians 5:23). When Moses left the dwelling of his father-in-law, he made provision for his family: "And Moses took his wife and his sons, and set them upon an ass, and he returned to the land of Egypt" (Exodus 4:20a). In the process of time: "When Jethro, the priest of Midian, Moses' father in law, heard of all that God had done for Moses, and for Israel his people, and that the LORD had brought Israel out of Egypt; Then Jethro, Moses' father in law, took Zipporah, Moses' wife, after he had sent her back, And her two sons; of which the name of the one was Gershom; for he said, I have been an alien in a strange land: And the name of the other was Eliezer; for the God of my father, said he, was mine help, and delivered me from the sword of Pharaoh: And Jethro, Moses' father in law, came with his sons and his wife unto Moses into the wilderness, where he encamped at the mount of God: And he said unto Moses, I thy father in law Jethro am come unto thee, and thy wife, and her two sons with her" (Exodus 18:1-6).

Moses Decided to Wake Up and Live when he moved beyond his human flesh, with all of his excuses about not being equipped enough, the people will not believe him, and asking God to send

another. God spoke to him about hearing the cries of his people, seeing their tears, and knowing their sorrows. Therefore, eventually Moses made his journey into Egypt to deliver the people of Israel from the hands of Pharaoh and his taskmasters; so they could serve the Lord. Within this deliverance, there were ten plagues, and the last one entailed the death of the Egyptians' firstborn, both of the people and their animals: "And he called for Moses and Aaron by night, and said, Rise up, and get you forth from among my people, both ye and the children of Israel; and go, serve the LORD, as ye have said" (Exodus 12:31). The main reason for the children of Israel being delivered from Egypt, was to "serve the Lord." So often God's people want to be delivered from situations – "Is it to serve the Lord or oneself?" After the children of Israel fled from Pharaoh's house, his people began to speak into his ear; they told Pharaoh that the children of Israel were gone and for him to rethink the matter of letting the Israelites go: "And it was told the king of Egypt that the people fled: and the heart of Pharaoh and of his servants was turned against the people, and they said, Why have we done this, that we have let Israel go from serving us" (Exodus 14:5)?

This passage of Scripture, speaking into the leader's ear, exemplifies a very familiar passage with the chief priests and Pharisees speaking in Pilate's ear about the death of Jesus: "Saying, Sir, we remember that that deceiver said, while he was yet alive, After three days I will rise again" (Matthew 27:63). Therefore, to soothe Pilate, the governor's uneasiness and suspicions, he had guards to watch and make sure the sepulchre was sealed: "Pilate said unto them, Ye have a watch: go your way, make it as sure as ye can. So they went, and made the sepulchre sure, sealing the stone, and setting a watch" (verses 65, 66). When word got out that Jesus's tomb was empty, the people assembled with the elders to make bribe the soldiers in order to put the blame on Jesus' disciples, because they wanted to be protected by Pilate and not be at fault in their duty, while sleeping as guards in watching the sepulchre of Jesus: "And when they were assembled with the elders, and had taken counsel, they gave large money unto the soldiers, Saying, Say ye, His disciples came by night, and stole him away while we slept. And if this come to the governor's ears, we will persuade him, and secure you. So they took the money, and did as they were taught: and this saying is commonly reported among the Jews until this day" (Mathew 28:12-15).

Moses' journey eventually led him in the wilderness for forty years with a rebellious nation; the Israelites, and Moses ultimately did not go over to Canaan, the Promised Land, with his people. Some people say: "Oh, it is so bad that Moses did not carry a rebellious nation to the Promised Land." But oh how the late Rev. Dr. Benjamin Elijah Mays prophetically orchestrates one's understanding: "This was the thing that kept Moses alive: the dream, the goal, the ideal, reaching for the stars and grasping after the moon. Abolish the dream, destroy the ideal, blot out the vision- you kill the man, whether he be 17, 21, 25, 50, or 100" (Mays, 1969, p. 121).

Neither Moses nor the people of God can be content when God hears the cries of His people. "No, No, No, I have heard, I have seen, and I know about my people." A Moses, a Joshua, a Saul, a Stephen, a Peter, a Paul, a leader, a laity, a child will be raised up to deliver God's people out of bondage!

Historical Leaders Raised Up By The Lord

During times of slavery in the United States many cried out for God to send them "a Moses" to deliver them out of the bondage of slave catchers, slave masters, and slave drivers. God heard their cry and raised up "a Moses" - Harriet Tubman, who was called "The Moses of her People." Harriet was not much over five feet tall; she was illiterate, spoke dialect, and was the youngest of her siblings like Moses in the Bible. The Adlerian theory of Dr. Alfred Alder, a psychotherapist and psychiatrist gives emphasis to birth order and the relationship of siblings. In regards to Moses and Harriet being the youngest, the theory states: "Youngest children will never be dethroned ..... Often, they will use their observations to develop in areas and ways that none of their siblings have attempted and often they will outshine all of their brothers and sisters" (Bitter, 2009, p. 103). This theory does emphasize the lives of Moses and Harriet. Harriet made nineteen trips back into slavery where she rescued some three hundred slaves out of the bondage of slavery. One of the differences between Harriet Tubman and Moses is that Harriet did not look at her deficiencies as making her inadequate, slow speech, inquiring about who sent her, emotional hurdles or rejections of the people, like Moses did. Harriet knew and readily accepted that she was chosen by God to deliver her people out of slavery.

The Lord continued to raise up "a Moses." Frederick Douglass, an illiterate boy, would trick the little boys into teaching him how to write: "When I met any boy who I knew could write, I would tell him I could write as well as he... With these, I learned mainly how to write" (Douglass, 1986, p. 87). With this knowledge, Frederick put words together, which eventually led to his escape from slavery. When Douglass heard that his master (some say his biological father) – "The whisper that my Master was my father" (p. 49.) was on his deathbed, he went to visit him. The name "Frederick Douglass" has gone down in the pages of history as an abolitionist, advocate for mankind, writer (describing his life as a slave), etc. Whereupon, after toiling with the cruelty of slavery and being hampered in his efforts to change the laws, Abraham Lincoln was raised up by God to be the president of the United States and issued the Emancipation Proclamation which declared "that all persons held as slaves" within the rebellious states "are, and henceforward shall be free."

Langston Hughes, a creative-minded individual and a prolific writer, took up the pen to write about a character: "He is my ace-boy, Simple" (viii). The character Simple would stand on the street corner or sit in the bar talking about the injustice, great contributions of his race, relationships, leaders in positions of authority, the church, church folks, and life-living situations that would cause one to raise an eyebrow with awe!

Baldwin (1963), wrote a profound letter entitled *My Dungeon Shook: Letter to My Nephew on the One Hundredth Anniversary of the Emancipation* to his nephew, James who was named after him. The letter was written on the one-hundredth anniversary of the Emancipation. Portrayals in the letter come from where his nephew came from – the livestock of slaves that toiled in the midst of obstacles. He encouraged his nephew to believe that he, too, could weather the storms of life: "It will be hard, James, but you come from sturdy, peasant stock, men who picked cotton and dammed rivers and built railroads, and, in the teeth of the most terrifying odds, achieved an unassailable and monumental dignity. You come from a long line of great poets, some of the greatest poets since Homer. One of them said, *The very time I thought I was lost, My dungeon shook and my chains fell* off" (p. 24). This prolific writer, with a creative mind, wrote about the church and saints. A lot of Baldwin's writings of the church comes from his own experiences. This prolific writer brings in scenes of being on the mourning bench, having your sins purged, prayer meetings all night (shut-ins), living in a house where the husband/father portrays one personality at church and another personality at home: "Well, he is dead, he never saw you, and he had a terrible life; he was defeated long before he died because, at the bottom of his heart, he really believed what white people said about him. This is one of the reasons that he became so holy" (p. 18). It is without reservation, that I submit to all young Black males to read the letter and reap the benefits of survival of their race.

Benjamin Elijah Mays was born with two biblical names – **Benjamin**, meaning "son of the right hand," and **Elijah**, meaning "Yahweh is God." (In the Bible when Rachel was dying, she named her son Benoni, meaning "son of my sorrow," but his father, Jacob renamed him Benjamin). The name of this visionary, educator, trailblazer, and theologian, the Rev. Dr. Benjamin Elijah Mays, somewhat coincides with the meaning of the word "Yahweh," one of the names of God. Mays's name has gone down through the pages of history with many titles: honor student, author, recipient of a doctoral degree, Dean of the School of Religion at Howard University, spokesman, preacher, President of Morehouse College, prolific writer, and the person who delivered the eulogy of Dr. Martin Luther King, Jr: "To be honored by being requested to give the eulogy at the funeral of Dr. Martin Luther King, Jr., is like asking one to eulogize his deceased son-so close and so precious was he to me" (Mays, 1968, p. 9). Prior to his upstream life, he states: "As a child my life was one of frustration and doubt" (Mays, 1971, p. 35). Benjamin was only allowed to have four months of school, and Afterward he had to return to the farm. He was not content with this situation. Mays (1971) exemplifies his character as a man born to rebel against the odds and obstacles of life that tends to impede one's progress, destiny, and determination. He became rebellious with his father, stating that he could not go back to the farm and that he must attain an education. Mays was not rebellious like some youths and adults today. He was rebellious because he wanted to achieve a much higher calling to be an educated man who had something to offer himself and to society as a whole.

I Woke Up One Day & Decided to LIVE!

The Rev. Dr. Benjamin Elijah Mays words of counsel, wise wisdom, and a life-living perspective

"The tragedy of life doesn't lie in not reaching your goal. The tragedy lies in having no goal to reach. It isn't a calamity to die with dreams unfulfilled, but it is a calamity not to dream. It is not a disaster to be unable to capture your ideal, but it is a disaster to have no ideal to capture. It is not a disgrace not to reach the stars, but it is a disgrace to have no stars to reach for. Not failure, but low aim is sin" (Mays, 1969, p. 120).

> **Author's Personal Note:** I would love to see the late Rev. Dr. Benjamin Elijah Mays name more prominent in a visual way. He was such a prolific and realistic writer about life-living situations. Unfortunately, too many people have not heard about this great man of God.

Therefore, Benjamin held on to his belief about receiving an education, in spite of his father's repeated words – "Weren't there only two honest occupations for Negro men – preaching and farming" (Mays, 1971, p. 36)? As his son stepped out on faith, telling his father that he would not return to the farm, his father became angry: "When Father saw that I was determined to go to a better school, and knew that I had to have money in order to do so, he angrily threw a ten-dollar bill at me. So I made my way to Orangeburg without Father's blessing but with my mother's prayers" (p. 38). In the midst of Benjamin's turmoil, he would often pray, asking God to move out "every hindrance and cause" that kept him from achieving his dream of being educated. Later in Rev. Dr. Benjamin Elijah May's life, he "thanked God" for not moving his father out of his life, who at first did not see his son's dream, his son's potential, and why he was not content with staying on the farm and only receiving four months of schooling. Mays did not look at his inadequate finances for his education or housing. His focus was on striving to achieve an education.

The true story of Solomon Northup, which was formulated into a movie *12 Years A Slave,* depicts scenes of the cruelty of slavery. Prior to gathering around the graveyard, Eliza, a slave who often cried and shared tears, was told by Plat, a slave: "Stop crying!" She responded with tears and grief, asking him a question: "Do you cry for your children?" He could not answer her with a "yes." His main objective was "survival." Later at the graveyard, Plat joined in singing the Negro Spiritual, *Roll Jordon Roll*, as he fellowshipped with the saints. When Patsey, a slave, returned to the plantation, she received a severe beating by Plat and the master. Afterward, Plat saw the pain and tears in her eyes. This is when he shared tears of both of their pains and sorrows of slavery. Somewhat later, a stranger showed up on the plantation as a builder and Plat put his trust in him, asking if he would write to his friends in the north about his situation. It was not until the tears of Plat that God moved on his behalf of deliverance through a stranger of trust. Afterward, while working in the field, a familiar face showed up to claim "freedom" for Plat. The sheriff asked Plat: "Do you know this man?" Plat looked, identified the man and ran to him for refuge (https://www.youtube.com/watch). The Lord heard Plat's prayer, saw his tears, and knew his hardship with his taskmasters. Therefore, after twelve years, Solomon (Plat) was delivered out of slavery and reconciled with his friends and family.

The Lord continues to raise up "a Moses" to deliver his people out of the perils of one's life. For God's servants today, as it was for God's servants in the Bible, there can be no contentment when the cries of God's people are calling out for deliverance.

Moral – Biblical and Life-Living:
My contentment will not override the cries, tears, and sorrows of God's people

---

Discussion Questions

In regards to one's calling, some preachers say: "I ran from my calling." Do you believe this saying comes from Moses' experience when God called him to "go" into Egypt? What are some of the reasons people run from their calling in ministry?

As a Believer of Jesus Christ, you have prayed, cried out, and sought the Lord for your deliverance, and to no avail has deliverance come. You have also had "prayer warriors" praying, and it seems like the Lord has not heard your cries, seen your tears, or know your sorrows. What do you do?

In this chapter, it gives some non-biblical persons raised up by the Lord. How do you see yourself as a leader used by God?

Case Study:
You are overseeing a large ministry and you feel in your spirit the Lord is calling you to a much smaller ministry that is out of state. The flesh in you does not want to take this ministry because you do not know the people, plus it will definitely hurt you and your family financially. You are a spiritual person and you know the voice of the Lord. At this time, the flesh and the spirit are at war with each other: "For the flesh lusteth against the Spirit, and the Spirit against the flesh: and these are contrary the one to the other: so that ye cannot do the things that ye would" (Galatians 5:17).

Prayerful Reflection

Dear Father,
Thank You for your patience with me and others who act as though You don't know us better than we know ourselves. Help us to set aside our insecurities and humbly accept the call You've placed upon us. Help us to release our anxiety as we remember that Your strength is made perfect in our weakness.

Samson, A Judge of Israel

An Opportunity to Sport, Turned Into a Day of Vengeance

"And Samson called unto the LORD, and said, O Lord GOD, remember me, I pray thee, and strengthen me, I pray thee, only this once, O God, that I may be at once avenged of the Philistines for my two eyes."

Judges 16:28

After the death of Joshua, Moses' successor, the Lord raised up judges where the people took their disputes and concerns: "Nevertheless the LORD raised up judges, which delivered them out of the hand of those that spoiled them" (Judges 2:16). Samson, a Nazarite (consecrated or devoted) to God by birth, could not cut his hair, drink wine, strong drink, nor eat unclean things. He was one of the judges of Israel: "And he judged Israel in the days of the Philistines twenty years" (Judges 15:20). Samson was like some people in Biblical times, and like many of us today – he fell by giving in to his weakness, and his enemies; the Philistines devoured him.

In hindsight, Samson's failure entailed ungodly women. He married an uncircumcised Philistine, he took a harlot, and he loved a woman named Delilah. When Samson saw one of the daughters of the Philistines, he told his parents: "Get her for me; for she pleaseth me well" (Judges 14:3b). His parents tried to deter their son's thinking process, in asking him realistically: "Is there never a woman among the daughters of thy brethren, or among all my people, that thou goest to take a wife of the uncircumcised Philistines?" (verse 3a) Samson would not take heed to wise counsel from his parents. His mind was made up to have a wife that "pleases him well." With Samson being the couple's only child and his mother being barren prior to Samson's birth, this may have caused the parents to side with their son's desire: "And the angel of the LORD appeared unto the woman, and said unto her, Behold now, thou art barren, and bearest not: but thou shalt conceive, and bear a son. Now therefore beware, I pray thee, and drink not wine nor strong drink, and eat not any unclean thing: For, lo, thou shalt conceive, and bear a son; and no razor shall come on his head: for the child shall be a Nazarite unto God from the womb: and he shall begin to deliver Israel out of the hand of the Philistines" (Judges 13:3-5). It was unfortunate that Samson fell into the hand of his enemy, since the angel said that he would deliver his people out the hand of the enemy – the Philistines.

Samson's enemy, the Philistines, tried to destroy him and ultimately wanted him killed, so they looked for his weakness. At Samson's wedding, he gave a riddle and looked for it to be solved. Nobody was able, until the enemy threatened Samson's wife to get her to make her husband reveal the riddle: "Entice thy husband, that he may declare unto us the riddle, lest we burn thee and thy father's house with fire:" (Judges 14:15b). Again, the Philistines tried to launch their attack. When Samson was with the harlot, they: "laid wait for him all night in the gate of the city, and were quiet all the night, saying, In the morning, when it is day, we shall kill him" (Judges 16: 2b). Samson, in his supernatural strength, made an escape, with the mercy of God. Romans 6:1 asks: "WHAT shall we say then? Shall we continue in sin, that grace may abound?" The question is answered: "God forbid. How shall we, that are dead to sin, live any longer therein?" (verse 2). Samson, the judge, lived a life for pleasure. From a counseling theory perspective, he lived in the "here and now." Samson became foolish and his enemies laid by to seize the opportunity to capture him.

Samson, A Judge of Israel

The Bible does not mention that Samson loved his wife: "And Samson's wife wept before him, and said, Thou dost but hate me, and lovest me not" (Judges 14:16a). As a matter of fact, when Samson found out that his wife told the answer to the riddle, he called her a "heifer": "And he said unto them, If ye had not plowed with my heifer, ye had not found out my riddle" (verse 18c). Afterward, "But Samson's wife was given to his companion, whom he had used as his friend" (verse 20). Nor did Samson love the harlot that he was with till the midnight hour: "THEN went Samson to Gaza, and saw there an harlot, and went in unto her" (Judges 16:1). In the process of time, Samson tried to have a sexual relationship with his wife – (Does this sound familiar with an ex-spouse – not all, "some")? But, her father said, he can't have her: "BUT it came to pass within a while after, in the time of wheat harvest, that Samson visited his wife with a kid; and he said, I will go in to my wife into the chamber. But her father would not suffer him to go in" (Judges 15:1).

For Delilah, the story is different for Samson regarding loving a woman. The Bible says that Samson "loved a woman in the valley of Sorek, whose name was Delilah" (Judges 16:4b). Delilah's name means *"Delight." She* was hired by the Philistines, and paid by each one of them to deceive Samson into telling her where his strength came from: "And the lords of the Philistines came up unto her, and said unto her, Entice him, and see wherein his great strength lieth, and by what means we may prevail against him, that we may bind him to afflict him: and we will give thee every one of us eleven hundred pieces of silver" (verse 5). Delilah did not have to do any physical harm to Samson. She had him in a position to deceive him, because he fooled around and fell in love with her – an ungodly woman. Elvin Bishop's song, *Fooled Around and Fell in Love says*, "*I must have been with about a million girls.*" Samson didn't go through a million girls. According to Scripture, he went through three women, and the one he fell in love with cost him the high price of being captured by his enemies, losing both of his eyes, being put into prison, and ultimately losing both the one he loved, Delilah, and his own life.

The Philistines found where Samson's heart lay: with a woman he loved – Delilah. Jeremiah 17:9 says: "The heart is deceitful above all things, and desperately wicked: who can know it?" Samson still allowed his pleasures to control him, and it made him foolish. Samson's heart and his danger grew alongside each other.

Man's Root of Temptation and Weakness for Women

From a Biblical perspective, temptation and weakness of men for women did not start nor stop with Samson, the Judge. It started with Adam, the first man in the Garden of Eden. This temptation and weakness of men for women comes in many forms from Satan. In the Garden of Eden, Satan's temptation came through a serpent to the weaker vessel - the woman. Some people have said in a humorist way regarding "The Six Days of Creation": "There may have been a reason God created woman last" - Created her while man slept!: "And the LORD God caused a deep sleep to fall upon Adam, and he slept: and he took one of his ribs, and closed up the flesh instead thereof; And the rib, which the LORD God had taken from man, made he a woman, and brought her unto the man" (Genesis 2:21, 22). In the Garden of Eden, the Lord gave a command to Adam: "And the LORD God commanded the man, saying, Of every tree of the garden thou mayest freely eat: But of the tree of the knowledge of good and evil, thou shalt not eat of it: for in the day that thou eatest thereof thou shalt surely die" (Genesis 2:16, 17). Adam was obedient in the beginning to this command, and he had no qualms about being alone in the Garden of Eden; until the Lord saw differently and began to form living creatures. Afterward, the Lord mentioned: for Adam there was not found an help meet for him (verse 20a), so He caused woman to be with Adam. The temptation and weakness of man has presented itself ("MAN that is born of a woman is of few days, and full of trouble" Job 14:1) since: "And when the woman saw that the tree was good for food, and that it was pleasant to the eyes, and a tree to be desired to make one wise, she took of the fruit thereof, and did eat, and gave also unto her husband with her; and he did eat" (Genesis 3:6). Afterward, God came walking in the garden and called to Adam: "And the LORD God called unto Adam, and said unto him, Where art thou" (verse 9)? The LORD God did not call for Eve, He called for Adam; whom he left in charge.

King David fell into his weakness of adultery with Bathsheba: "And it came to pass in an eveningtide, that David arose from off his bed, and walked upon the roof of the king's house: and from the roof he saw a woman washing herself; and the woman was very beautiful to look upon. And David sent and enquired after the woman. And one said, Is not this Bathsheba, the daughter of Eliam, the wife of Uriah the Hittite? And David sent messengers, and took her; and she came in unto him, and he lay with her; for she was purified from her uncleanness: and she returned unto her house. And the woman conceived, and sent and told David, and said, I am with child" (2 Samuel 11:2-5). With this news, King David used every tactic he could to cover up his sin by getting Bathsheba's husband, Uriah, to sleep with his wife (this way, it could be said that Bathsheba's husband was the father and not David. This same deceitfulness is manifested in today's society). David told Uriah to go to his house and wash his feet, had him come to his house and got him drunk; but because Uriah wouldn't go to Bathsheba because his comrades were still in battle, David's tactics didn't work.

Therefore, since none of David's tactics worked, he relinquished to his final plan to have Uriah killed: "And he wrote in the letter, saying, Set ye Uriah in the forefront of the hottest battle, and retire ye from him, that he may be smitten, and die" (2 Samuel 11:15). David's plan worked: "And the shooters shot from off the wall upon thy servants; and some of the king's servants be dead, and thy servant Uriah the Hittite is dead also" (verse 24). It has often been said: "Your sins shall find you out." Then God sent the prophet Nathan unto David to speak "what thus saith the Lord." The prophet used a scenario of two men living in the same city – one rich, and the other poor. After the scenario, David was emotional: "And David's anger was greatly kindled against the man; and he said to Nathan, As the LORD liveth, the man that hath done this thing shall surely die: And he shall restore the lamb fourfold, because he did this thing, and because he had no pity" (2 Samuel 12:5, 6).

The prophet Nathan exposed David's hidden sins: "And Nathan said to David, Thou art the man" (2 Samuel 12:7a). Afterward, the prophet reminded David of the things the Lord has done for him, and if those things were not enough, the Lord would have done more for him. Because of the Lord's mercy, David did not die in his sin. However, there were consequences for his sins of adultery and murder: "the sword shall never depart from thine house" (verse 10a), "Thus saith the LORD, Behold, I will raise up evil against thee out of thine own house, and I will take thy wives before thine eyes, and give them unto thy neighbour, and he shall lie with thy wives in the sight of this sun" (verse 11), "For thou didst it secretly: but I will do this thing before all Israel, and before the sun" (verse 12), and "the child also that is born unto thee shall surely die" (verse 14b). King David accepted the consequences for his sins, repented, and the Lord put away his sins: "And David said unto Nathan, I have sinned against the LORD. And Nathan said unto David, The LORD also hath put away thy sin; thou shalt not die" (verse 13).

King Ahab sinned when he married Jezebel, a king's daughter, and when he started to serve and worship Baal: "And Ahab the son of Omri did evil in the sight of the LORD above all that were before him. And it came to pass, as if it had been a light thing for him to walk in the sins of Jeroboam the son of Nebat, that he took to wife Jezebel the daughter of Ethbaal king of the Zidonians, and went and served Baal, and worshipped him. And he reared up an altar for Baal in the house of Baal, which he had built in Samaria. And Ahab made a grove; and Ahab did more to provoke the LORD God of Israel to anger than all the kings of Israel that were before him" (1 Kings 16: 30-33). Maybe, just maybe Ahab was thinking when he married Jezebel, since he is a king, he would marry a king's daughter, and they would have a great "union in marriage," where each "being a king" and "coming from a household of a king," would bring about "like minds." Some people say: "likes attract," while others say, "opposites attract."

When King Ahab wanted to purchase Naboth's vineyard, he approached him as a businessman in a negotiable way: "And Ahab spake unto Naboth, saying, Give me thy vineyard, that I may have it for a garden of herbs, because it is near unto my house: and I will give thee for it a better vineyard than it; or, if it seem good to thee, I will give thee the worth of it in money" (1 Kings 21:2). Naboth would not sell his vineyard to the king because it was forbidden by the Lord; he inherited it, and it was most likely sentimental to him: "And Naboth said to Ahab, The LORD forbid it me, that I should give the inheritance of my fathers unto thee" (verse 3). Afterward, the king went home discouraged, and retreated to bed with no food. His wife wanted to know what was troubling him, and he started wimping his discouragement to her: "And he said unto her, Because I spake unto Naboth the Jezreelite, and said unto him, Give me thy vineyard for money; or else, if it please thee, I will give thee another vineyard for it: and he answered, I will not give thee my vineyard" (verse 6).

After his wife carefully listened to her husband's concerns, she reminds him of who he is and she took her position (not title) as wife, where she took matters into her own hands: "And Jezebel his wife said unto him, Dost thou now govern the kingdom of Israel? arise, and eat bread, and let thine heart be merry: I will give thee the vineyard of Naboth the Jezreelite. So she wrote letters in Ahab's name, and sealed them with his seal, and sent the letters unto the elders and to the nobles that were in his city, dwelling with Naboth" (I Kings 21:7, 8). Upon receiving word of the death of Naboth, this controlling wife, Jezebel, had no remorse. She basically told her husband to man-up and uphold his title as king: "And it came to pass, when Jezebel heard that Naboth was stoned, and was dead, that Jezebel said to Ahab, Arise, take possession of the vineyard of Naboth the Jezreelite, which he refused to give thee for money: for Naboth is not alive, but dead" (verse 15). In today's vernacular, one would call King Ahab a "jelly back man with no backbones." He had the title "King," and his wife, Jezebel, put herself in the "position" - running things. The enemy does not care anything about one's "title," he focuses on the "position." Some people in the Body of Christ are so concern about "titles" and "positions."

From a Biblical perspective, Herod's wife, Herodias was so concerned about her position as "first lady" being taken away, that she took advantage in an evil way of an opportunity to work for her good. After John the Baptist gave the prophetic word to King Herod: "For John said unto him, It is not lawful for thee to have her" (Matthew 14:4), his wife, Herodias made her move through her daughter. During the king's birthday celebration, Herodias' daughter danced so well, that she pleased King Herod and he told her: "But when Herod's birthday was kept, the daughter of Herodias danced before them, and pleased Herod. Whereupon he promised with an oath to give her whatsoever she would ask. And she, being before instructed of her mother, said, Give me here John Baptist's head in a charger" (verses 6-8).

Usually, children from controlling parent(s) will replicate the behavior of control and will make few visits home as adults. In replicating parent(s) behavior of control, it is not good in marriages and can seriously cause contention in their marriage; where one person has a dominant and controlling behavior, and the other is passive. It can become a war zone with a high possibility of ending up in divorce court which in turn, increases the high rate of divorce. The movie, *Sleeping with the Enemy*, is a prime example of a "control person." Laura wanted to come under her controlled husband, Martin; until she faked her death, changed her name, and moved to another state. Truth warrants itself that when some people are in controlled relationships, they may eventually take a walk and keep on walking, without looking back. They will not be like Lot's wife in the Bible, where she looked back and dissolved away: "But his wife looked back from behind him, and she became a pillar of salt (Genesis 19:26). In a couple of scenes in the movie after leaving her husband, Laura unconsciously noticed how she still allowed her husband to continue controlling her, as she continued to line-up bath towels and food cans. When she realized this behavior, she disorganized the bath towels and food cans.

It is mind-boggling that some church folks will try to control some people in the Body of Christ by putting them on a "guilt trip." A prime truth entails at some churches when women will put on a little make-up and lipstick (don't let the lipstick be red!), some of the saints would tell the women: "You're looking like a Jezebel!" These saints were sincere in their own way; while at the same time, they got it all wrong. The Bible specifically says, that when Jezebel heard that King Jehu was coming to town: "she painted her face, and tired her head, and looked out at a window" (2 Kings 9:30b). It was this author's learned knowledge of Jezebel many years' later, that saints are dealing with a spirit, and not a person. The Jezebel spirit is a "take over spirit." During a time of full-time ministry, it was said to a person: "If I ever see your pastor. . ." The person did not give time to complete the sentence, but chimed in with: "My pastor made me head over this . . ." In completing the sentence to the person, it would have been said (did not get a chance): "You do not have a spirit of humanity – you have a take over spirit." During this time of outreach ministry, it was very rare that a pastor called to see how their people were doing in ministry, and what they were teaching. Sometimes, pastors have to be a "show up pastor," and come unannounced and unexpected, like the second coming. It is the author's belief that periodically (at least once per year), pastors should have a conversation with the person where their church provides ministries outside of their church. If not, one can put their ministry in Danger, Danger, Danger.

Williams (2002) has expanded one's knowledge of Jezebel and this spirit. Prior to the pastor writing his book, *The Jezebel Spirit: Freeing Yourself from the Spirit of Control*, somebody put Francis Frangipane's book, *The Jezebel Spirit,* on his desk (which he read), and it blessed him. This book enlightened Pastor Williams to see this spirit of control, manipulation, witchcraft, and other facets of the Jezebel spirit; which ultimately led him to pick up the pen and write, where he continues one's enlightenment of the Jezebel spirit.

Jezebel's tragic, with her own people; the eunuchs throwing her out the window, reminds one of an old saying: "It's your own that will take you down." King Jehu wanted to know who was on his side, and if so, do what he said: "And he lifted up his face to the window, and said, Who is on my side? who? And there looked out to him two or three eunuchs. And he said, Throw her down. So they threw her down: and some of her blood was sprinkled on the wall, and on the horses: and he trode her under foot" (2 Kings 9:32, 33). The eunuchs were most likely at their wits end in dealing with Jezebel, with her controlling, manipulating, and witchcraft spirit; so they took heed to answer Jehu, the King, when he wanted to know: "who was on his side, who?"

While King Jehu was enjoying his meal and drink, he thought about Jezebel's father, who was a king. Therefore, he said: "Go, see now this cursed woman, and bury her: for she is a king's daughter" (2 Kings 9:34a). But oh, it was too late to bury Jezebel. The dogs had enjoyed their meal – eating Jezebel. The only things left of this cursed woman was her skull, feet, and the palms of her hands. The prophetic word of Elijah, the prophet came to pass: "And of Jezebel also spake the LORD, saying, The dogs shall eat Jezebel by the wall of Jezreel" (1 Kings 21:23). The woman, Jezebel is dead; but the spirit of controlling, manipulating, witchcraft, and other related facets are still alive in some churches, church folks, marriages, families, supervisors, co-workers, etc. A person once named three women of an extended family who appears to control their husbands. After hearing the names, there were no refutes to the insight.

Some of the Israelites destroyed themselves, when they fell into their weakness with women, and worshipped other gods: "AND Israel abode in Shittim, and the people began to commit whoredom with the daughters of Moab. And they called the people unto the sacrifices of their gods: and the people did eat, and bowed down to their gods" (Numbers 25:1, 2). Balak, king of the Moabites, was afraid and distressed because the Israelites had grown in number. To ease his fear and distress, he hired Balaam, the prophet to curse God's people: "And Moab was sore afraid of the people, because they were many: and Moab was distressed because of the children of

Israel. And Moab said unto the elders of Midian, Now shall this company lick up all that are round about us, as the ox licketh up the grass of the field. And Balak the son of Zippor was king of the Moabites at that time. He sent messengers therefore unto Balaam the son of Beor to Pethor, which is by the river of the land of the children of his people, to call him, saying, Behold, there is a people come out from Egypt: behold, they cover the face of the earth, and they abide over against me: Come now therefore, I pray thee, curse me this people; for they are too mighty for me: peradventure I shall prevail, that we may smite them, and that I may drive them out of the land: for I wot that he whom thou blessest is blessed, and he whom thou cursest is cursed" (Numbers 22: 3-6). The Lord enquired of Balaam who these men were and told him not to go with them. Balaam did not take heed. It took an ass to show Balaam his disobedience: "And the LORD opened the mouth of the ass, and she said unto Balaam, What have I done unto thee, that thou hast smitten me these three times" (verse 28)?

The Lord presented a parable with oracles, and Balaam received wise counsel from the Lord to give Balak. Balak, the Moabite eventually became emotionally distressed in not being able to defeat his fear and distress in having the Israelites cursed, so he retreated: "And Balak's anger was kindled against Balaam, and he smote his hands together: and Balak said unto Balaam, I called thee to curse mine enemies, and, behold, thou hast altogether blessed them these three times" (Numbers 24:10). Therefore, since Balak was not able to have his enemies cursed, and Balaam blessed Israel three times; the two departed from each other: "And Balaam rose up, and went and returned to his place: and Balak also went his way" (verse 25). The saints will often say: "I'm blessed and highly favor." The enemy is not about defeat, and he fights dirty. He is lurking and will use every trick and tactic in the book to try and destroy the people of God. He will pull something out of his hat, and you won't know what hit you.

The end result, takes an emotional self-examination in asking oneself questions: "What was I thinking, where was my mind, how did I allow myself to get caught up in my weakness?" The Bible reminds one: "if it were possible, they shall deceive the very elect" (Matthew 24:24b). Satan is not always the scapegoat for one's shortcoming – Sometimes it's "us." Therefore, one can imagine Satan periodically pouting and saying: "I get blamed for everything." In Flip Wilson's scapegoat for blaming somebody, he would say: "The Devil made me do it." "Do we blame Satan for allowing one to fall into their weakness, or do we take ownership in allowing ourselves to fall into our weakness"?

After some expiration of time after Balak's and Balaam's departure from each other, some of the children of Israel fell into their weakness – women and worshipping other gods. In other words, "they destroyed themselves." The children of Israel did to themselves what Balaam and others could not do. "How often do those in the Body of Christ fall into their weakness"? The Israelites decision caused God to make a judgment call: "And Israel joined himself unto Baalpeor: and the anger of the LORD was kindled against Israel. And the LORD said unto Moses, Take all the heads of the people, and hang them up before the LORD against the sun, that the fierce anger of the LORD may be turned away from Israel. And Moses said unto the judges of Israel, Slay ye every one his men that were joined unto Baalpeor" (Numbers 25:3-5). In the interim of slaying the people, it took Phinehas to stay God's hand of the plague upon the Israelites. The saints will often say: "Lord, stay your hand": "Phinehas, the son of Eleazar, the son of Aaron the priest, hath turned my wrath away from the children of Israel, while he was zealous for my sake among them, that I consumed not the children of Israel in my jealousy" (verse 11). Later, Moses sent the Israelites against the Midianites, and Balaam was killed (see Numbers 31).

I Woke Up One Day & Decided to LIVE!

Finally, Delilah said: "How canst thou say, I love thee, when thine heart is not with me" (Judges 16:15b)? After Delilah kept pressing Samson (his wife pressed him to tell her the riddle. Now, Delilah is pressing him – women pressing the leader. It's ironic the men couldn't press Samson, but the women could; the weaker vessel) to tell her the truth, he revealed his secret to the woman he loved, without considering or caring about the consequences: "And she made him sleep upon her knees; and she called for a man, and she caused him to shave off the seven locks of his head; and she began to afflict him, and his strength went from him" (verse 19). Love is powerful, especially when love and danger are intertwined. Luther Ingram's – oldie but goodie song, *If Loving You Is Wrong, (I Don't Want to Be Right)* applies to Samson. Even though this song is singing about been with a "married woman," Samson fell in love with his enemy. It was wrong for Samson to love Delilah, because she was an ungodly woman. She was paid by each one of the Philistines to destroy and ultimately kill him. They did not kill him. Samson asked to die with his enemy: "And Samson said, Let me die with the Philistines. And he bowed himself with all his might; and the house fell upon the lords, and upon all the people that were therein. So the dead which he slew at his death were more than they which he slew in his life" (verse 30). Samson didn't want to be right in been in love with Delilah. He didn't care about the consequences or his future. On the other hand, "could it be Samson felt untouchable"? In truth and reality, Samson loved Delilah – Love of a woman over the love of God!

He could lay his head on her lap and tell her all about his day - triumphs, troubles, and woes. Long (1998) gives a segment of what men don't want: "But there are things about Delilah that NO man wants! No man wants a woman who will connive with other men against him. No man wants a manipulative woman. No man wants a woman who will project herself as something she isn't. No man wants a woman who nags him day and night for what she wants. No man wants a woman who will betray him" (p. 30, 31). He also highlights how a Delilah is there to hear his stories without talking about what he did not do or say, the arguments, her dissatisfactions with him, etc. Proverbs, the book of wisdom, states: "It is better to dwell in the corner of the housetop, than with a brawling woman and in a wide house" (Proverbs 25:24). A Delilah will not be brawling. She will make a man feel cared for, make him feel needed, make him feel important, and make him feel like he's on the mountain, even when he's in the valley. A Delilah will not have him hold her for the night, nor allow herself to fall in love with him. She will make him feel like he is somebody special. On the other hand, some wives only look at their spouses' faults, their own discouragements with him, speak about how Brother John treats his wife better, bills, children acting out, etc.

A Delilah is not trying to point out all his faults, woes, and shortcomings. She can make him lay his head on her lap and tell her all about his troubles, which can at the moment, take him away from the cares of his world. A person once said in a secret talk to their best friend: "I like dating them married men. They'll give you their undivided attention." Samson was not married to Delilah - she was his mistress. He gave her his undivided attention, and for awhile he found peace, a safe haven, and a place of refuge. But to God, this relationship was taboo; and in the end this real-life situation ended in ruin. I am reminded of one of my favorite shows as a child, *Lost In Space*. In the proximity of trouble, the robot saw trouble with the Robertson's sitting on the picnic table outside of the ship. The robot would say: "Danger, Danger, Danger... Danger Will Robertson!" The Robertson's would ignore the robot and continue their enjoyment of fellowship; while Dr. Smith, with that smirk look on his face sided up with the enemy because he wanted so badly to get back home. He also confided with the robot his plans to do whatever it took to make it back home, even if it meant befriending the enemy. Delilah was a "Danger, Danger, Danger!" A pastor preached a message entitled: "Be careful where you lay your head."

Samson, the judge was in the position where he listened to people's troubles, concerns and issues in general. But who heard his stories, and where could he take his concerns? As leaders, one can be in the crowd of people while seeking refuge for their own situations, and yet be lonely and miserable at the same time. At a church meeting one night, the preacher for the night got up and said: "I'm the most blessed man here." Some women in the congregation knew where he was going and unimaginably longed for God to bless them in that endeavor. The preacher had his wife to stand up. Afterward, he asked her: "Turn around so the people can see you." She turned around, smiled, and waved at the people. Oh how some of the women applauded this couple. A few years later, this same pastor was in a conversation with someone and the person reflected back on the preacher's words: "The most blessed man here." The pastor responded: "Yea, married and miserable." The person said, "What?" The "what" came back with: "You know; you been married before." The person tried to get the preacher to talk on it, but he only changed the subject. Paul Laurence Dunbar's poem *We Wear The Mask* "We wear the mask that grins... But let the world dream other-wise" (p. 71). This poem reflects the outer appearance of what some people want others to see, but in reality the real person is under the mask.

Samson, the judge maybe didn't have anyone to hear his stories but Delilah. His parents did not agree with the person he chose to marry. Therefore, why would they approve of Delilah? Due to Samson's strength and his reputation for killing that he carried in his community, people were afraid of him. This judge, Samson, was physically strong; yet he was morally weak when it came to women.

Whatever the reason for Samson seeking refuge in Delilah and her making him sleep upon her knees, brought comfort to each in their own way. Samson didn't care about anything but getting what he wanted, and Delilah was paid for her service by each one of the Philistines.

We read on three occasions that Delilah told Samson: "The Philistines be upon thee, Samson" (Judges 16:9, 12, 14). Some people would say: "Duh, Samson, that woman is setting you up." Samson was blinded by his love for Delilah. Percy Sledge's song, *When a Man Loves a Woman* says: "If she's playing him for a fool, he's the last to know." Delilah knew and the Philistines knew that they were playing Samson for a fool. The last to know was Samson. Therefore, Delilah played Samson for a fool and afterward she received her money by each one of the Philistines: "But the Philistines took him, and put out his eyes, and brought him down to Gaza, and bound him with fetters of brass; and he did grind in the prison house" (verse 21).

Samson had lost a lot, but he **Woke Up and Decided to Live when the opportunity presented itself.** A banquet took place with the Philistines, and they sent for Samson to "sport them": "And it came to pass, when their hearts were merry, that they said, Call for Samson, that he may make us sport. And they called for Samson out of the prison house; and he made them sport: and they set him between the pillars" (Judges 16:25). Samson did sport them. But in the midst of sporting them, he asked a lad to take him by the hand and lead him to the pillars: "And Samson said unto the lad that held him by the hand, Suffer me that I may feel the pillars whereupon the house standeth, that I may lean upon them" (verse 26). Isaiah 11:6 speaks about a child leading them. One can imagine Samson, incarcerated behind prison walls; going to the gym, the big yard, the small yard, and in his cell working out and building up his muscles to keep his image as one with strength. The Philistines remembered him in his strength and the banquet was getting boring, so they sought for some entertainment to liven things up! Samson's enemy – the Philistines meant it for his bad, when they called him out of prison to "sport them" - But God meant it for Samson's good.

Near the end of Samson's life, the scripture does not mention that he blamed Delilah for allowing herself to be used by his enemies, nor does it seem that Samson focused on the shoulds, coulds, woulds. He had a spirit of repentance and asked God for his strength back: "And Samson called unto the LORD, and said, O Lord GOD, remember me, I pray thee, and strengthen me, I pray thee, only this once, O God, that I may be at once avenged of the Philistines for my two eyes" (Judges 16:28). God granted Samson his prayer: "And Samson said, Let me die with the Philistines. And he bowed himself with all his might; and the house fell upon the lords, and upon all the people that were therein. So the dead which he slew at his death were more than they which he slew in his life" (verse 30). The parable of the widow woman and the unjust judge speaks about how she went to see an unjust judge with her request: "Avenge me of mine adversary" (Luke 18:3b). In other words: "work on my behalf." The unjust judge ignored her request; but because of her persistence with the unjust judge, he finally responded to her: "And he would not for a while: but afterward he said within himself, Though I fear not God, nor regard man; Yet because this widow troubleth me, I will avenge her, lest by her continual coming she weary me" (verses 4, 5). God answered Samson much more quickly. Samson's avenge came as he took advantage of the opportunity to call upon the Lord. The New Testament speaks about whose vengeance it is, and who will repay: "Dearly beloved, avenge not yourselves, but rather give place unto wrath: for it is written, VENGEANCE IS MINE; I WILL REPAY, saith the Lord" (Romans 12:19).

As born-again Believers of Jesus Christ, we too can call upon Him while He is near, pray without ceasing (without stopping), and take heed in knowing that the battle is not ours but the Lord's! Judge Samson finally won the battle with his prayer: "Only this once" to be avenged of his adversary – the Philistines.

Moral – Biblical and Life-Living:
A call out of prison to sport, gives one another chance to defeat the enemy

---

Discussion Questions

What are some of the ways Judge Samson had scales on his eyes for women, especially Delilah that caused him to lose so much?

Do you still see people's pattern of temptation and weakness for women/men in the church and society as a whole?

The people of God are a blessed and not a cursed people. Therefore, why do some of us keep falling into our weakness and continue to make the same mistakes (bad decisions) over and over again? We cannot continue to blame others, nor embark upon Flip Wilson's saying: "The Devil made me do it." The blaming started in the Garden of Eden with "shifting the blame." Adam blamed his wife: "And the man said, The woman whom thou gavest to be with me, she gave me of the tree, and I did eat" (Genesis 3:12), and Eve blamed the serpent; whom she said tricked her: "And the woman said, The serpent beguiled me, and I did eat" (verse 13b). Do husband and wife still blame each other today when they get caught up in things?

I Woke Up One Day & Decided to LIVE!

Do you believe the "Jezebel spirit" of controlling, manipulating, witchcraft, and other related facets are in the church today? If so, what can the saints do?

Are people born evil, mean, or vindictive; or do they eventually become like that? (see Romans 1: 28-32) These people are "inventors of evil things" (verse 30b), and "have pleasure in them that do them" (verse 32b). Some people will help a person along the way with their needs, and at the same time; gossip about them, tell their business, and work against them. In truth, they are hoping the person will fall. It reminds one of an old realistic song of the O'Jays *Back Stabbers*.

Case Studies:
Some people in the Body of Christ are so focused on having a "title" and a "position," when the enemy could care less about titles and positions. Titles and positions are needed in the church, because things have to be organized with someone to oversee ministries. While at the same time, one can be so focused on titles and positions, and danger is all around them. This reminds one of a child playing outside and predators are all around them.

During a Bible study, the pastor was teaching, and in the midst his wife stood up and said: "No, that is not right pastor." Afterward, the church was mute, and the pastor eased back in the "pastor's chair." In the process of time, many members left the church and went elsewhere. The few members that stayed were not able to carry on financially, so the church doors were closed, with a padlock. Is an open forum warrant (talk about it), or do we let it be like water rolls off a duck's back?

Prayerful Reflection

Dear Father,
Thank You for providing new mercies everyday. Forgive me for the times I find myself allowing my desires to rule my life. Purge from me the inappropriate desires that caused Samson, Ahab, and David to sin. Help me to acknowledge my wrongdoing so I can be clean in Your sight. Remind me that You are the one in control and if I don't take authority over myself, my sins will take over me.

David, A Man After God's Own Heart

Encouraging Yourself in the Midst of Distress

"And David was greatly distressed; for the people spake of stoning him, because the soul of all the people was grieved, every man for his sons and for his daughters: but David encouraged himself in the LORD his God."
1 Samuel 30:6

David, the son of Jesse and the youngest of his siblings, like Moses, was a man chosen by God to lead his people, Israel. The name David means "well-beloved." He was a shepherd boy, an organized musician, a worship leader, a writer of Psalms, a man of war, a king, and a man after God's own heart: "And Samuel said to Saul, Thou hast done foolishly: thou hast not kept the commandment of the LORD thy God, which he commanded thee: for now would the LORD have established thy kingdom upon Israel for ever. But now thy kingdom shall not continue: the LORD hath sought him a man after his own heart, and the LORD hath commanded him to be captain over his people, because thou hast not kept that which the LORD commanded thee" (1 Samuel 13:13, 14).

Saul, Israel's first King, followed his own mind as a leader. He was a disobedient king, who did not follow the instructions of Samuel, the prophet, or the Lord. The straw that broke the camel's back for this disobedient king was when Samuel asked him if he had done everything the Lord told him to do, and Saul concurred he did. Afterward, the prophet heard animal noise: "And Samuel said, What meaneth then this bleating of the sheep in mine ears, and the lowing of the oxen which I hear" (1 Samuel 15:14)? The king began to justify his behavior in a twisted way, using Biblical principles about sacrifice: "And Saul said, They have brought them from the Amalekites: for the people spared the best of the sheep and of the oxen, to sacrifice unto the LORD thy God; and the rest we have utterly destroyed." (verse 15). The prophet responded in a scolding and questionable way to this disobedient king: "Wherefore then didst thou not obey the voice of the LORD, but didst fly upon the spoil, and didst evil in the sight of the LORD" (verse 19)? The end result of King Saul's justifying came with stern words from the prophet, Samuel: "For rebellion is as the sin of witchcraft, and stubbornness is as iniquity and idolatry. Because thou hast rejected the word of the LORD, he hath also rejected thee from being king" (verse 23).

In being disobedient to the Lord, it carries a lot of weight, and the end results can be devastating and everlasting. Oftentimes as a child growing up, when I was disobedient to my mother, she would tell me: "Girl, you just have your own mind." King Saul, like some leaders today, have their own mindset in seeing things from their personal lens and finite mind. The Lord may keep them in a leadership position, but His anointing may not be with them. A pastor once said in his message: "God is the only one that will keep you working when you have been fired." Saul was fired and still in position as king, and God's anointing was not with him as king. David was not recognized as king while King Saul was in the position. The Lord raised up one leader at a time: "And when he had removed him, he raised up unto them David to be their king; to whom also he gave testimony, and said, I HAVE FOUND DAVID THE SON OF JESSE, A MAN AFTER MINE OWN HEART, which shall fulfill all my will" (Acts 13:22); "Then came all the tribes of Israel to David unto Hebron, and spake, saying, Behold, we are thy bone and thy flesh. Also in time past, when Saul was king over us, thou wast he that leddest out and broughtest in Israel: and the LORD said to thee, Thou shalt feed my people Israel, and thou shalt be a captain over Israel. So all the elders of Israel came to the king to Hebron; and king David made a league with them in Hebron before the LORD: and they anointed David king over Israel. David was thirty years old when he began to reign, and he reigned forty years. In Hebron he reigned over Judah seven years and six months: and in Jerusalem he reigned thirty and three years over all Israel and Judah" (2 Samuel 5:1-5).

Throughout David's life, along with his triumphs, he also had many hurdles that caused difficult detours in his life. In spite of the hurdles with people working against him, one son; Amnon raped his half-sister, Tamar; another son, Absalom, rebelled against him, and having his brother killed; the contention of King Saul's hatred and jealousy towards him, and his own ungodly and unwise decisions along the way; grace, mercy and favor were given David. In the midst of David giving in to his human flesh, he found his way back to God with a spirit of repentance and seeking the will and the face of God. The contention of Saul's hatred and jealousy towards David did not start until the women elevated David for slaying more than Saul and the king's kingdom was at risk of being taking away: "And the women answered one another as they played, and said, Saul hath slain his thousands, and David his ten thousands. And Saul was very wroth, and the saying displeased him; and he said, They have ascribed unto David ten thousands, and to me they have ascribed but thousands: and what can he have more but the kingdom? And Saul eyed David from that day and forward" (I Samuel 18:7-9). Prior to David going against the giant Goliath, the Philistine; King Saul gave David his weapons: "And Saul armed David with his armour, and he put an helmet of brass upon his head; also he armed him with a coat of mail" (I Samuel 17:38). But young David intercepted with the king's weapons because God wanted a witness in the battle against their enemy: "And David said unto Saul, I cannot go with these; for I have not proved them. And David put them off him." (verse 39b). After David slew the Philistine and the women cheered David, King Saul's hatred and jealousy began and carried on, with contention between the two men. This king was so focused on his hatred and jealousy of David, that he could not stay focus on his calling and position as Israel's first King in leading God's people. This behavior can manifest itself in ministries today, where one is so focused on external things, that they miss the mark of their calling in ministry.

A person once said in their prayer to the Lord as they anointed themselves with blessed oil: "Lord I want to be great in you!" The Lord came back in a scolding manner with a question: "Do you know what you're asking for?" Again, with a sincere heart, this person prayed again: "Lord I want to be great in you!" The Lord's second response was the same scolding question: "Do you know what you're asking for?" The person stayed on their knees in prayer with the same request: "Lord I want to be great in you!" This time, the Lord was quiet, with no response. So often, people have a great zeal to launch out in the deep for the Lord, without a clue of the spiritual battles they will face with the enemy, with people in their company, with some "church folks," and with people in general. Ephesians 6:10-20 speaks about spiritual battles and what armour to put on – The Whole Armour of God; trust, the breastplate of righteousness, the gospel of peace, shield of faith, the helmet of salvation, and the sword of the Spirit.

Leaders are often those on the front line, where people depend on them to take their leadership role and responsibilities. When David and his men returned to Ziklag, their houses were burned down and their wives and children were taken captive: "So David and his men came to the city, and, behold, it was burned with fire; and their wives, and their sons, and their daughters, were taken captives" (1

Samuel 30:3). The Amalekites had taken the people captive but did not kill them: "Then David and the people that were with him lifted up their voice and wept, until they had no more power to weep" (verse 4). Afterward, these same folks flipped the script on David, and in cahoots, spoke of stoning him. Therefore, David received a backlash from the people: "And David was greatly distressed; for the people spake of stoning him, because the soul of all the people was grieved, every man for his sons and for his daughters: but David encouraged himself in the LORD his God" (verse 6). This situation is similar to Jesus' triumphal entry into Jerusalem, where the people waved palms and cried out in praise: "And many spread their garments in the way: and others cut down branches off the trees, and strawed them in the way. And they that went before, and they that followed, cried, saying, HOSANNA; BLESSED IS HE THAT COMETH IN THE NAME OF THE LORD: Blessed be the kingdom of our father David, that cometh in the name of the Lord: Hosanna in the highest" (Mark 11:8-10). But before the week was over, folks cried out to Pilate, the Governor: "And they cried out again, Crucify him... And they cried out the more exceedingly, Crucify him" (Mark 15: 13, 14b). The Word says that the enemy comes in two ways: as an angel of light; to deceive (see Revelation 20:10), and as a roaring lion; to destroy (see 1 Peter 5:8). One could consider the people were an angel of light trying to deceive Jesus by welcoming him, and they were a roaring lion when they cried out: "Crucify him."

David's men were not the only ones greatly distressed because of the captivity. David's two wives, Ahinoam and Abigail, were taken captive also, and he grieved for them and others. The men that spoke about stoning David were distressed because of their sons and daughters, not their wives. It's interesting how they did not mention their distress with their "wives" taken captive. To counteract their distress, somebody had to be blamed, which led to "stoning." A person can stone another person verbally and physically. Verbally, they can stone with "gossip." The epistle of James says it well about the tongue: "Even so the tongue is a little member, and boasteth great things. Behold, how great a matter a little fire kindleth! And the tongue is a fire, a world of iniquity: so is the tongue among our members, that it defileth the whole body, and setteth on fire the course of nature; and it is set on fire of hell. For every kind of beasts, and of birds, and of serpents, and of things in the sea, is tamed, and hath been tamed of mankind: But the tongue can no man tame; it is an unruly evil, full of deadly poison" (James 3:5-8). The late Rev. James Cleveland mildly says about the tongue, in a prelude to the song *Breathe On Me*: "They mean well, but they just have a gossiping nature." Therefore, the saints have to pray: "Lord, shut up the gang sayers mouths" (people with ungodly gospel). In many churches on Sunday morning, there was a "testimony service." This part of the service has been dropped, cut back, or replaced in some churches. The reason for needing this change, some said, was that some testifying tended to "share a little gossip," or took advantage of the opportunity to get back at someone with whom they had a discord. To alleviate this poor witness, one church replaced the testimony service with "praise dancers." A Christian comedian said in her talk on stage: "I'm not gossiping, I'm sharing."

It is unfortunate that some witness entails "hidden agenda" in the Body of Christ. The sin of iniquity (disobedience to the Lord) crept in and weakness took its toll. It was a spiritual fight with the spirit and the flesh fighting against each other: "the spirit indeed is willing, but the flesh is weak" (Matthew 26:41b). After deliverance, the enemy tried to raise its head to rekindle sin. But oh no, deliverance came with: "I'm not the ......" The sinful person took the microphone and nonverbally said: "I'll get you back." Oh how sin manifested itself with a twist of reading from the holy writ and "grinning and sinning," as Valerie Boyd sings. Oh, how the congregation gave their amen, hallelujah, thank you Jesus; while the other sat quietly in the pulpit like a mouse and asked the Lord, "How can ungodly stuff go on right in the pulpit?" In the Bible, when King Solomon prayed, he called sin out and after he finished praying: "the glory of the LORD filled the house" (2 Chronicles 7:1b). God's glory will not fill the house when there is ungodly stuff in the House of God – Sin in the Camp.

Physically, people can pick up stones to throw at a person. After Stephen, the deacon, gave the historical facts about the forefathers in order to condemn the Jewish leaders: "Then they cried out with a loud voice, and stopped their ears, and ran upon him with one accord, And cast him out of the city, and stoned him: and the witnesses laid down their clothes at a young man's feet, whose name was Saul" (Acts 7:57, 58). Stephen did not pick up those same stones to throw back at the people. He interceded for the people, and had a spirit of forgiveness: "And he kneeled down, and cried with a loud voice, Lord, lay not this sin to their charge. And when he had said this, he fell asleep" (verse 60).

The people did not say when they were going to stone David. David only knew that he was in the midst of distress, and that he was being blamed for the situation. Therefore, he "encouraged himself in the LORD his God" (1 Samuel 30: 6b). We do not know how David encouraged himself in the Lord. With him being a cunning musician, did he play a musical instrument? As a writer of Psalms, did he pick up the pen to write? Being a man after God's own heart, did he lay his supplications out before the Lord in prayer? Whichever way David encouraged himself in the Lord, he rescued himself from the stoning of the people. Oftentimes when people threaten or gossip about people, many in return act on their emotions and the situation can escalate to a fight; somebody can get hurt, and even killed – "out of sight, out of mind." The criminal justice system is filled with volatile emotions, where people are on a tether, parole, probation, house arrest, community service, or in prison while serving years or life. A prisoner that was dismissed from a program could not return to the general population, because "all beds" were filled with 1,600+ incarcerated prisoners. Therefore, the prisoner had to wait until a prisoner was released from prison, so he could return to the general population. From a ministry point of view, we need strong and willing outreach ministries, along with preventive methods in the community, and ministries that will take heed to Biblical principles (see Jeremiah 3:15; Luke 14:23). David did not allow himself to fall into the trap of the enemy, by allowing his emotions to erupt when the people blamed him for the fire and captivity.

Once while traveling, I backed my car from a parking spot in the parking lot. As I backed up, a car was coming down toward me. When I drove off, a lady yelled from out her window: "You need to learn how to drive!" I kept driving and said to myself: "I'll let that go." If born-again Believers of Jesus Christ are not prayed up, they can be caught up in the flesh and allow things to escalate to high-risk situations that can result in harmful behavior. When Jesus was in the Garden of Gethsemane, he took three of his disciples - Peter, James, and John and asked them to pray for one hour while he went up further to pray. The disciples' eyes were too heavy for prayer. After two attempts of trying to get the disciples to pray, Jesus relinquished Himself: "And he cometh the third time, and saith unto them, Sleep on now, and take your rest: it is enough, the hour is come; behold, the Son of man is betrayed into the hands of sinners. Rise up, let us go; lo, he that betrayeth me is at hand" (Mark 14:41, 42). When Judas Iscariot, the betrayer, and his company came to arrest Jesus, Peter reacted in the flesh, drew out his sword, and cut the man's right ear off. If Peter had been prayed up, and not caught up in his flesh, he would have stayed in the spiritual realm when the call was made to pray for "one hour." It is unfortunate that, "the power of prayer" is not always implemented by some Believers, who confess Jesus Christ as their Lord and Savior. Prayer is a powerful weapon that the Lord has given to the saints. It does not cost money, title, or position. However, it does call for a person's time.

One can imagine David saying to the people who formed an alliance against him: "You are carnal-minded people. I'm not going down like this in the midst of my distress, being blamed for the situation, and facing your threat of stoning me. It is time for me to go into spiritual warfare and ask the priest's son for the ephod": "And David said to Abiathar the priests, Ahimelech's son, I pray thee, bring me hither the ephod. And Abiathar brought thither the ephod to David" (1 Samuel 30:7). The ephod served as guidance for David when the threat of "being stoned" by the people. An ephod is a priestly garment, that David wore in his dance: "And David danced before the LORD with all his might; and David was girded with a linen ephod" (2 Samuel 6:14). McGee (1982) elaborates more on the ephod and how it was used: "It had two stones, one on each shoulder, on which were engraved the names of the twelve tribes of Israel: six on one shoulder and six on the other. In other words, the high priest came to the altar of prayer bearing Israel on his shoulders" (p. 183). Wow, such a spiritual encounter on one's shoulders!: "And thou shalt take two onyx stones, and grave on them the names of the children of Israel: Six of their names on one stone, and the other six names of the rest on the other stone, according to their birth" (Exodus 28:9, 10).

I Woke Up One Day & Decided to LIVE!

> **12 Tribes of Israel: Genesis 35:23-26; 1 Chronicles 2:1-2**

Reuben	Gad
Simeon	Asher
Levi	Issachar
Judah	Zebulun
Dan	Joseph
Naphtali	Benjamin

After the ephod was brought to David, he asked God two questions: "Shall I pursue after this troop? shall I overtake them?" (1 Samuel 30:8a). The Lord answered him immediately: "Pursue: for thou shall surely overtake them, and without fail recover all" (verse 8b). It is imperative that leaders wear the proper garments and seek the Lord's guidance as they pursue their leadership positions. David was on the front line as he and other men began to pursue their enemies. In the midst of the journey, some of the men were not able to pursue the journey. They remained behind while the leader, David, and those that were able continued to pursue their enemies.

In the midst of pursuing their enemies, David and the men had no trail or idea where their enemies were. God gave them 'a ram in the bush' as they came upon a wounded Amalekite servant. He was no good for his company, so they had left him for dead, but he was of good use to David and his company. He gave them valuable information in telling them where their enemies were, with a swear that they would not kill him, nor turn him over to his master: "And David said, unto him, To whom belongest thou? and whence art thou? And he said, I am a young man of Egypt, servant to an Amalekite; and my master left me, because three days agone I fell sick. We made an invasion upon the south of the Cherethites, and upon the coast which belongeth to Judah, and upon the south of Caleb; and we burned Ziklag with fire" (1 Samuel 30:13, 14). David and his company located the Amalekites, smote them, and took their spoil (leftover). The Bible says: "the wealth of the sinner is laid up for the just" (Proverbs 13:22b). Because some of the men were so faint and not able to pursue the journey, the men that were able to pursue the journey felt that the "faint men" should not receive the spoil. But the leader, David, spoke up on their behalf: "Then said David, Ye shall not do so, my brethren, with that which the LORD hath given us, who hath preserved us, and delivered the company that came against us into our hand" (1 Samuel 30:23).

A situation arose that caused this man, David, to be in the midst of distress, where he began to seek the Lord's direction. As he went into spiritual warfare, seeking the Lord's direction; his distress of being stoned turned into recovering all, with the help of a wounded enemy. David and his company recovered their wives, children, belongings, and the spoil of their enemies.

David was a leader that stayed focused in the midst of his distress. **He Woke Up and Decided to Live when he "encouraged himself in the LORD his God" (1 Samuel 30:6b).** He did not let the people detour him with their threat of "stoning him." Being on the front line as a leader can bring a heavy weight to one's shoulders. Oftentimes, leaders are the first to be blamed when things go wrong; some people will not take ownership in asking themselves: "Did I play a part in the situation?" David, a leader called by God, upheld his responsibilities in this situation by not giving in to their threat. He followed through as a leader, and in the end, they were all blessed with the spoil of their enemies - even those who were not able to make the journey. A leader must stay strong in the midst of distress and seek God's guidance; as they pursue the journey God has called them to.

Moral – Biblical and Life-living:
Words of being stoned, will not distress the leader in me.

I Woke Up One Day & Decided to LIVE!

Discussion Questions

One old childhood saying: "Sticks and stones may break my bones, but words will never hurt me." Words can cut a person like a knife. Do words hurt when folks lie, gossip, and spread false accusations about you?

Some members at the church formed a coalition – "an alliance between two people or entities, often against a third" (Bitter, 2009, p. 413) against their pastor. These church members are faithful in coming to church every Sunday. To help the pastor alleviate some of the confusion, he sums it up by saying: "I just preach over folks." How do you preach over church members trying to destroy you and hating you at the same time? David's response to the threat of being stoned was to "encourage himself in the Lord his God." As someone said: "You got to get a crazy praise!"

David's own men came together and spoke of stoning him. How do you handle people in the Body of Christ coming together to work against you, vote you out, shun you, smile in your face and stab you in your back? Do you go into spiritual warfare, or do you fight in the flesh? In the movie, *Color Purple*, the two sisters were outside talking and hanging clothes on the line when the kids ran through the clothes. Nettie told her sister, Celie that she can't let them do her like that. That she has to fight. Celie responded honestly that she didn't know how to fight. Some people in the Body of Christ are not willing to be honest in saying, "they don't know how to fight." This fighting also applies to some married couples, where they fight in the flesh, (holding back on their spouse, silent treatment, hidden agendas, etc.) and not in the spirit. Ephesians 6:12 reminds Believers who they are fighting against: "For we wrestle not against flesh and blood, but against principalities, against powers, against the rulers of the darkness of this world, against spiritual wickedness in high places."

Some people are so eager to be in leadership positions, without proper garments. What are some of the spiritual garments leaders need to wear?

Some of the men with David were so faint and not able to continue the journey, so they were left behind. Therefore, the men with David believed that the men should not receive the spoil (leftover), because they did not fight in the battle with the Amalekites. How do you handle a situation when some people believe that people should not receive something, and you believe differently as a leader?

Case Study:
The choir has practiced for two consecutive weeks for a musical concert, and Sister Johnson has not attended one rehearsal because she claims she has been ill. On the day of the musical concert, she states she is feeling better, and is ready to lead her favorite song that is often requested by many people in the church. Sister Johnson knows all the songs, because she has led most of them in the past.

Prayerful Reflection

Dear Father,
There are so many times when distress overwhelms me. In frustration, others might become angry enough to, in a manner of speaking, stone me. Help me to respond like David and seek You. Help me to continue by following Your guidance so that I may see victory. Help me to remember that those who may be weak and faint around me should be blessed to receive Your merciful blessings, just as those who fought alongside me.

Incarcerated Prisoners, A Person that Allows Their Destiny to Unfold

I Just Can't Sit Here and Die

"And there were four leprous men at the entering in of the gate: and they said one to another, Why sit we here until we die? If we say, We will enter into the city, then the famine is in the city, and we shall die there: and if we sit still here, we die also. Now therefore come, and let us fall unto the host of the Syrians: if they save us alive, we shall live; and if they kill us, we shall but die."

2 Kings 7:3, 4

"And as he entered into a certain village, there met him ten men that were lepers, which stood afar off: And they lifted up their voices, and said, Jesus, Master, have mercy on us. And when he saw them, he said unto them, Go shew yourselves unto the priests. And it came to pass, that, as they went, they were cleansed."

Luke 17:12-14

The Talented Tenth (1903) essay by Dr. W.E.B. DuBois states: "The Negro race, like all races, is going to be saved by its exceptional men. The problem of education, then, among Negroes must first of all deal with the Talented Tenth; it is the problem of developing the Best of this race that they may guide the Mass away from the contamination and death of the Worst, in their own and other races" (https://en.wikipedia.org/wiki/The_Talented_Tenth). "Du Bois used the term 'the talented tenth' to describe the likelihood of one in ten black men becoming leaders of their race in the world, through methods such as continuing their education, writing books, or becoming directly involved in social change"

I Woke Up One Day & Decided to LIVE!

(https://en.wikipedia.org/wiki/Social_change). Therefore, this author reflects on the question that is often posed to prisoners: "Are you doing time, or is time doing you?" One end of the spectrum to this question challenges prisoners to use their gifts, talents, skills, abilities, creative mind (in a healthy way), linking up with people moving into their destiny, making one's acquaintance with the law library, and with the prisoner law clerks (who are often most knowledgeable in legal issues). The other end of the spectrum allows one to go down memory lane with the shoulds, coulds, woulds, throwing the buck, and blaming others – "If it wasn't for you, you weren't there for me, I was not loved by my parent(s)." The cause of blaming started in the Garden of Eden, when Adam blamed Eve, his wife: "And the man said, The woman whom thou gavest to be with me, she gave me of the tree, and I did eat" (Genesis 3:12). In return, Eve blamed the serpent: "The serpent beguiled me, and I did eat" (verse 13b). The list of blaming can be endless. These emotional distortions tend to bring about emotional distress, mental and personality disorders, little to no reconciliation with family and loved ones, a spirit of unforgiveness, etc.

In the Old Testament, when a person had leprosy, a cancer-like disease, they had to leave their family, friends, and community and go live in isolation. The priest had the responsibility to pronounce a person "unclean" and to isolate them from their family and the community: "He is a leprous man, he is unclean: the priest shall pronounce him utterly unclean; his plague is in his head. And the leper in whom the plague is, his clothes shall be rent, and his head bare, and he shall put a covering upon his upper lip, and shall cry, Unclean, unclean. All the days wherein the plague shall be in him he shall be defiled; he is unclean: he shall dwell alone; without the camp shall his habitation be" (Leviticus 13:44-46).

Incarcerated Prisoners, A Person that Allows Their Destiny to Unfold

"If we say, We will enter into the city, then the famine is in the city, and we shall die there: and if we sit still here, we die also. Now therefore come, and let us fall unto the host of the Syrians: if they save us alive, we shall live; and if they kill us, we shall but die" (2 Kings 7:4). The dialogue with these isolated men of leprosy was surrounded with the question "If." "If we say... if we sit still here... if they save us alive... if they kill us (verse 4). The word "if" is a small word, yet carries faith and responsibilities, which can allow a person to launch out into the deep. 2 Chronicles 7:14 speaks of the four prerequisites of God's people – humble themselves, pray, seek my face, and turn from their wicked ways; then the three blessings shall follow – hear from heaven, forgive their sin, and heal their land. Another "if" of prerequisite, is the abiding: "If ye abide in me, and my words abide in you, ye shall ask what ye will, and it shall be done unto you" (John 15:7). So often people want to receive the blessings of the Lord, yet His blessings are based upon conditions. Usually in Biblical passages, the "if" follows "then." A lot of breakthrough in one's life is wrought by stepping out in faith. Hebrew 11:1 gives the definition of faith: "NOW faith is the substance of things hoped for, the evidence of things not seen."

After being isolated from their family, community and loved ones; these men went into a dialogue, looking at their situation of being isolated. One can imagine them periodically reminiscing about been at home, in their own community, and providing for their family. These men wanted to be providers as one can reflect on 1 Timothy 5:8 "But if any provide not for his own, and specially for those of his own house, he hath denied the faith, and is worse than an infidel."

Let's use our imaginations here, in order to picture this dialogue between these men

I Woke Up One Day & Decided to LIVE!

"John, you and I came to this place of isolation about five years ago. Wow, how time flies. I sure miss my daughter, Zina. My wife, Susan was pregnant when cancer-like sores came upon me. My Zina should be starting school, and I wanted to be there to take her on the first day." John looks sad and disappointed because he is missing an opportunity to be a provider and protector to his family, and it is his hope that Susan will await his return and Zina will have a chance to know her father. "Man I know how you feel about family. I never had children, but I have four siblings and at times we had our disagreements. As I look things over, I wish I had been more kind to my baby sister. Often times, she got on my nerves because she came to me for advice. I would shun her at times and talked mean to her. I pray God will give me another chance to make things right with her." Samuel chimed in: "You act like it is over for us. It's not over till God says it's over. I have faith to believe things will change. As we sit here and talk about 'if,' we'll sit here and die. We have to step out in faith and put it into action." "You're right Samuel; it is time to step out in faith. As a matter of fact Samuel, your name means 'Ask of God,' and let us men, with this disease of leprosy, ask God to make us whole, make provision for us to return to our family, loved ones, and our community with a new disposition on life."

In today's society, because of mass incarceration, prisoners are isolated from the community, family, and loved ones; often due to bad decisions, seeking refuge and love in wrong places, falling into one's weakness, and a host of other misfortunes. Unfortunately, some people in relationships do not know how to say goodbye in a healthy way; therefore, since they do not, they keep singing Gladys Knight & The Pips song *Neither One Of Us (Want To Be The First To Say Goodbye)*, until they stay too long and things turn into a "heat of passion/love-hate relationship," the flesh kicks in, and an "Oops" happens that formulates into a "victim of crime." At the end of one's sentence, many ex-offenders will return to the community and show themselves worthy of being a productive citizen in society. The downward spiral with some, unfortunately, equals a revolving door – back in prison on installments (in prison 2 years, make parole, don't report to probation officer, back in prison, do another 2 years, make parole, get out of prison, you and baby mama have an argument and you slap her, she calls the police, you go back to prison and complete your sentence). A 3-10 year sentence, ends up being 10 years served in prison, when one only had to do 3 years. When one puts something in the layaway, they pay on it until the balance is paid in full. An old and truthful saying: "When you know better, you do better." If not, the saying of Motel 6 can apply: "We'll leave the lights on for you."

Ex-offender is a word that seems to be used too loosely in the community. I was at an outreach ministry gathering, and the speaker asked: "When will we get past introducing - This is John, an ex-offender?" He submitted this word "ex" to the audience: "How would you like to be introduced – This is John, Mary's ex-spouse, ex-boyfriend/ex-girlfriend, ex?" The audience became mute, when they heard his question that may have hit home to some. A very familiar Biblical passage of being reminded and accused of one's past is: "And the scribes and Pharisees brought unto him a woman taken in adultery; and when they had set her in the midst, They say unto him, Master, this woman was taken in adultery, in the very act... So when they continued asking him, he lifted up himself, and said unto them, He that is without sin among you, let him first cast a stone at her (John 8:3, 4, 7). When the mob were ready to stone a woman caught in adultery, Jesus stooped down and wrote on the ground (we don't know what Jesus wrote): "And they which heard it, being convicted by their own conscience, went out one by one, beginning at the eldest, even unto the last: and Jesus was left alone, and the woman standing in the midst" (verse 9).

In reality, when one reflects upon their own life, they have no stones to throw, nor can they refer to people as somebody's ex. Years prior, my heart was filled with joy when I mentioned to a person that a church in the community was growing with new members, people were getting saved, seeking the face of the Lord, and been delivered from substance abuse, criminal behaviors, promiscuity, and a host of other sinful behaviors. After patiently listening to me, the person went down memory lane with the ex-people of the church: "ex-prostitute, ex-drunk, ex-drug dealer, ex-abusers, etc." To bring matters home to all, I stated: "We all have our ex." Thankfully, our "ex-problems" are covered by the blood of the Lamb.

In the Old Testament, men with leprosy were not allowed to live in the community or with their family. These men were isolated and could not commune with their family or loved ones. This condition was beyond their control and their lot in life that they had to suffer with. Therefore, they had to make the best of a bad situation. Incarcerated prisoners are also separated from their family and loved ones. In the midst of separation, many have **Woke Up and Decided to Live when they allowed their destiny to unfold; where their hidden talents, skills, and abilities begin to be unfolded as musicians, artists, creative writers, published authors, advocates for themselves, others, and the likes.**

In the New Testament, we read about how Jesus cleansed ten lepers, who saw him afar off and cried out for mercy: "And as he entered into a certain village, there met him ten men that were lepers, which stood afar off: And they lifted up their voices, and said, Jesus, Master, have mercy on us" (Luke 17:12, 13). In Jesus having mercy, it can be something a person did wrong, and they need the Lord to intervene, or it can be something a person did not do which brought tragedy in their life. It was of no fault of their own that these men had leprosy. Mercy is what these men with leprosy cried out for. Mercy takes one back to what the Lord told Moses when he asked to see the Lord's glory: "will be gracious to whom I will be gracious, and will shew mercy on whom I will shew mercy" (Exodus 33:19b). Romans 9:15 is a reminder of mercy and compassion said to Moses: "For he saith to Moses, I WILL HAVE MERCY ON WHOM I WILL HAVE MERCY, AND I WILL HAVE COMPASSION ON WHOM I WILL HAVE COMPASSION." The ten men with leprosy were not consumed with the disease, because they chose to cry out for "mercy," versus "unclean, unclean." After their deliverance, they followed Jesus' instructions to go see the priest. Lamentations 3:22, 23 speaks about the Lord's mercy: "It is of the LORD'S mercies that we are not consumed, because his compassions fail not. They are new every morning: great is thy faithfulness." Some Believers are grateful for God's mercy, while others, in their gratefulness, will go the extra mile, and come back and say "Thank you Lord," like one of the ten lepers who was healed: "And one of them, when he saw that he was healed, turned back, and with a loud voice glorified God" (Luke 17:15).

The late Presiding Bishop G.E. Patterson's sermon on *CRAZY Praise Break* (Tape #943) illuminates on been delivered by a merciful God, and giving Him hallelujah praises: "But when I been in trouble, **and** when everything else has failed, **and** when I call on Jesus, **and** when He gives me the victory; get out of my way. **I got to** praise Him. **I got to** praise Him by lifting my hands. **I got to** praise Him in the dance. **I got to** praise Him with everything in me, because I've been delivered. Satan thought he had me, but I slipped through, one more time. **I got to** praise Him, because God brought me out. **I got to** praise Him, because He worked a miracle for me. **I got to** praise. . ." It is with sadness that some, after been released from prison (Egypt), with the mercy of the Lord, will not have a "CRAZY Praise Break," nor continue (although they served while incarcerated) to serve the Lord in the church or community. A comedian once said: "When some people go to prison, they find Religion - God, Buddha, Muslim, etc." It is a reality, thankless people applies across the board of humanity. They will accept the Lord's blessings and keep it moving. The Lord's blessings are based upon conditions. Remember that 2 Chronicles 7:14 gives the four prerequisites upon receiving the three blessings.

Therefore, if one is not thankful for God's mercy, an old saying may apply, "A hard head makes a soft behind." Sitting on the bunk, voices are replayed in the head (you are not psychotic) from mom, dad, teacher, preacher, aunt, uncle, strangers, and bystanders along the way; saying: "Don't fall into the enemy's trap, stay away from bad company, those people don't mean you no good, you need to leave them 'fast' or 'hot tail' girls alone, and boy, you was reared better than that, etc."; while another voice kicks in and ask questions: "Now where do I go from here, do I sit here and die, or do I pick up the torch and speak into my life and others; allowing myself to let my destiny unfold?" In the midst of sitting down and been away from the family, crowd, and one's familiarity; one can take heed to the crisis and embark upon the two characters of crisis from the Chinese: "The Chinese symbol for the word *crisis* is a composite of two characters: 'threat' and 'challenge' (not "opportunity," a common mistaken translation)" (Walsh, 2016, p. 7). This author poses the question, "Is it a threat to fall into the same trap, or is it a challenge to learn from one's bad decision(s)"?: "Trust in the LORD with all thine heart; and lean not unto thine own understanding. In all thy ways acknowledge him, and he shall direct thy paths" (Proverbs 3:5, 6). Oftentimes, one can use misfortunes as an opportunity to use the gifts, talents, skills, and abilities God had given them to turn things around for their good and for God's glory.

Incarcerated Prisoners, A Person that Allows Their Destiny to Unfold

Biblical and Reality Presents Itself with Isolation

Joseph's brothers exemplified several reasons for being jealous of him: his father Jacob (Israel) showed favoritism, Joseph told his brothers his dreams, and his father made his favorite son a coat of many colors: "Now Israel loved Joseph more than all his children, because he was the son of his old age: and he made him a coat of many colours" (Genesis 37:3). Jacob was only repeating the path of his parents regarding favoritism. All too well, some parents continue this path for various reasons: "And Isaac loved Esau, because he did eat of his venison: but Rebekah loved Jacob" (Genesis 25:28). "And when his brethren saw that their father loved him more than all his brethren, they hated him, and could not speak peaceably unto him" (Genesis 37:4). Therefore, to alleviate the dreamer and favoritism, the brothers came together in cahoots to get rid of their brother, Joseph: "And they said one to another, Behold, this dreamer cometh. Come now therefore, and let us slay him, and cast him into some pit, and we will say, Some evil beast hath devoured him: and we shall see what will become of his dreams" (verses 19, 20) – But God preserved Joseph. His brothers set him up for a blessing to bless them and to save his family and others from starvation. Years later, when Joseph revealed himself to his brothers, he had a spirit of forgiveness; he did not retaliate towards them. He upheld Biblical principles: "But as for you, ye thought evil against me; but God meant it unto good, to bring to pass, as it is this day, to save much people alive" (Genesis 50:20). The brothers told their father that his son, Joseph was alive and in a position of authority! "And told him, saying, Joseph is yet alive, and he is governor over all the land of Egypt. And Jacob's heart fainted, for he believed them not" (Genesis 45:26). Their brother Joseph was "Governor of Egypt" – Second in command to Pharaoh, who rose from "the pit to the palace," as some preachers preach: "And Pharaoh said unto Joseph, See, I have set thee over all the land of Egypt. And Pharaoh took off his ring from his hand, and put it upon Joseph's hand, and arrayed him in vestures of fine linen, and put a gold chain about his neck; And he made him to ride in the second chariot which he had; and they cried before him, Bow the knee: and he made him ruler over all the land of Egypt" (Genesis 41:41-43).

The movie, *Lion King*, depicts, Simba, overwhelmed with guilt and feeling responsible for Mufassa, his father's death, according to his uncle, Scar, who put Simba on the "guilt trip." Because of this, Simba left his family, friends, and community to be isolated and free from the worries, cares, and responsibilities; until the witch doctor, Rafiki meets up with him. Rafiki communicated to him the troubles with his family, and how his uncle, Scar, and his associates had taken over. Simba began to have a pity party, walking in circles, saying: "They don't need me, I started a new life, have new friends, etc." The witch doctor saw Simba's hurts from his past and stated: "Oh yes, the past can hurt. But from the way I see it, you can either run from it, or learn from it." In the midst of focusing on his distress in going down memory lane, the witch doctor knocked him in the head with his stick, and Simba said, "That hurts." The old folks would symbolically say: "Boy, you need some sense knocked in your head." The witch doctor replied: "It's supposed to hurt, your people need you!" The next time the witch doctor tried to knock him with his stick, Simba ducked, and he, his newly acquired friends, and the witch doctor removed themselves from isolation and headed back into Simba's community to take his responsibilities as king (www.ohmy.disney.com). Guilt and emotional distress can place a toll on one's endeavor to return to their community, but with a knock on the head, reality sets in. Many prisoners that are released from prison will return to their community, family, friends, and foes. The question is: "will one let the guilt, emotional distress, and gossip keep them from building up their community and being kings and queens in their community?" While in the past, some prisoners were participants in destroying their own community – Black-on-Black Crime.

From a Biblical perspective, Naomi is a prime example of someone leaving a bad situation, and going where the Lord visits his people in giving them bread after great loss: "Then she arose with her daughters in law, that she might return from the country of Moab: for she had heard in the country of Moab how that the LORD had visited his people in giving them bread" (Ruth 1:6). After Naomi lost her husband, sons, and daughters-in-law, she made a pivotal move to Bethlehem, the house of bread. When the people saw Naomi, the **busybodies** started with their **gossip** (see 2 Thessalonians 3:11, 12 on busybodies - meddlers in peoples business, without offering a helping hand). "So they two went until they came to Bethlehem. And it came to pass, when they were come to Bethlehem, that all the city was moved about them, and they said, Is this Naomi" (Ruth 1:19)? The epistle of James 3:5-8 says it so profoundly about the tongue: "Even so the tongue is a little member, and boasteth great things. Behold, how great a matter a little fire kindleth! And the tongue is a fire, a world of iniquity: so is the tongue among our members, that it defileth the whole body, and setteth on fire the course of nature; and it is set on fire of hell. For every kind of beasts, and of birds, and of serpents, and of things in the sea, is tamed, and hath been tamed of mankind: But the tongue can no man tame; it is an unruly evil, full of deadly poison." Therefore, the saints will say: "Lord, shut up the gang sayers mouths (ungodly gospel)."

Naomi looked at where she came from (a full life with a husband, sons, and daughters-in-law), to being (a widow and childless, except for daughter-in-law): "And she said unto them, Call me not Naomi, call me Mara: for the Almighty hath dealt very bitterly with me. I went out full, and the LORD hath brought me home again empty:

why then call ye me Naomi, seeing the LORD hath testified against me, and the Almighty hath afflicted me" (Ruth 1:20, 21)? Because of Naomi's misfortune, she did not want to be called Naomi (Pleasant), but called Mara (Bitter). According to Naomi, she left out full with a husband, two sons, and daughters-in-law; which probably made her financially stable and secure with the comfort of a family. With a detour in her life, Naomi knew she could not sit there and die. So she stepped out in faith, believing for betterment; in spite of her thinking the Lord was her enemy, and He had been bitter to her: "the hand of the LORD is gone out against me: (verse 13b). Unknown to her, the Lord had a ram in the bush and had ordered her steps through a kinsmen: "And Naomi said unto her daughter in law, Blessed be he of the LORD, who hath not left off his kindness to the living and to the dead. And Naomi said unto her, The man is near of kin unto us, one of our next kinsmen" (Ruth 2:20). Boaz, who was financially wealthy, owned fields, had servants, and was a kinsman, made provision for Naomi, Ruth, and generations to come.

The Talented Tenth essay *of Dr. W.E.B. Dubois,* which talks about becoming directly involved in social change. It involves going to one's family, communities, and churches to see needs and to implement ones' services, if the opportunity presents itself. If only more people, especially men after been released from prison will involve themselves in social change to embrace the church from a Biblical perspective in not been participants in letting anything prevail against the church – The *Ecclesia*, then John 6:38 will be more visible. If not, many are faced with the grief and sadness to see some churches being more about commercial (business), than spiritual (the Will of the sent one). Many years ago, at Convocation in Memphis, Tennessee, a preacher preached a Rhema word, which is still vibrant today: "If we don't do soul business, we'll be going out of business!" Therefore, as Believers of Jesus Christ, we must uphold the scripture: "And the lord said unto the servant, Go out into the highways and hedges, and compel them to come in, that my house may be filled" (Luke 14:23). Also, we must be busy about our Father's business in keeping the world abreast of the condition of their souls, so they will not spend eternity in hell where there is no hiding place and the lake which burns with fire and brimstone: "And the kings of the earth, and the great men, and the rich men, and the chief captains, and the mighty men, and every bondman, and every free man, hid themselves in the dens and in the rocks of the mountains; And said to the mountains and rocks, Fall on us, and hide us from the face of him that sitteth on the throne, and from the wrath of the Lamb: For the great day of his wrath is come; and who shall be able to stand?" (Revelation 6:15-17); "And in those days shall men seek death, and shall not find it; and shall desire to die, and death shall flee from them" (Revelation 9:6); "But the fearful, and unbelieving, and the abominable, and murderers, and whoremongers, and sorcerers, and idolaters, and all liars, shall have their part in the lake which burneth with fire and brimstone: which is the second death" (Revelation 21:8).

It appears that Satan and his angels are using God's own people to try to destroy the church by being more commercial than spiritual: "For there shall arise false Christs, and false prophets, and shall shew great signs and wonders; insomuch that, if it were possible, they shall deceive the very elect" (Matthew 24:24). Satan and his angels strive towards the head (leaders) to destroy the body (the church). An evangelist said during a revival service: "This is a great time for pastors," then he paused and spoke: "if you do ministry right." It is the author's belief that the evangelist was referring to people who are hurting financially, emotionally, and, spiritually from past and present hurts, distressful relationships, emotional cutoff (little to no contact with family – cut off like a faucet), subsystems (i.e. - six children – two talk to each other, two sparingly talk, one talks to all, and one doesn't talk to any siblings – black sheep of the family/identified patient), and other like matters. Therefore, if churches can help meet the needs of these hurts, to have ministries in place; then the Body of Christ can help eliminate some of the attacks of the enemy.

The late Abraham Maslow, Ph.D. was a psychologist, known for his "hierarchy of needs." One of the needs is a "sense of belonging." Most believers in the Body of Christ want to feel they belong to their church (not only as a member), and people care about them overall. Some former church members have said: "I stopped going to church because I don't feel a sense of belonging, nor cared for." In the midst of one's discomfort, they must be reminded to assemble themselves with the Body of Christ and the revelation of the church: "Not forsaking the assembling of ourselves together, as the manner of some is; but exhorting one another: and so much the more, as ye see the day approaching" (Hebrews 10:25); "And I say also unto thee, That thou art Peter, and upon this rock I will build my church; and the gates of hell shall not prevail against it. And I will give unto thee the keys of the kingdom of heaven: and whatsoever thou shalt bind on earth shall be bound in heaven: and whatsoever thou shalt loose on earth shall be loosed in heaven. Then charged he his disciples that they should tell no man that he was Jesus the Christ" (Matthew 16:18-20).

The commercial side of the church embraces more dollar lines, where it's communicated more about money - $100, $75, $50, $25, or whatever amount you have to bring; than prayer lines. You have unmarried saints sleeping with each other, having babies by leaders and others (not married to) in the church, one must buy a ticket to hear the word preached (gospel), some pastors and leaders preaching on the mountain top like two worlds coming together while living in the basement with sins of iniquity (disobedient to the Lord), leaders who only embrace certain folks in their circle, the usher who greets one with a welcome while at the same time gives one an offering envelope versus a "church bulletin" ("you can get that from our website"), taking more time to swipe a credit card versus praying for a distressed soul, more emphasis put on paying tithes and very little on being a good steward of what God has entrusted a person (some tithe payers will not pay their bills on time, pay people they owe, save $5.00 per month, or have a life insurance policy on themself), majoring in the minor – God ain't called no women to preach, and a host of other ungodly things going on in the church which takes the real meaning from the church – "And the lord said unto the servant, Go out into the highways and hedges, and compel them to come in, that my house may be filled" (Luke 14:23); "I can of mine own self do nothing: as I hear, I judge: and my judgment is just; because I seek not mine own will, but the will of the Father which hath sent me" (John 5:30).

Some church folks seeking their own will and not the Lord's will, has caused best-selling authors to pick up the pen to write and publish books about "church folk's business." Some of these best-selling authors are not always making up stories from their creative mind. They are using some actual situations – "the names have been changed to protect the identity." A visiting pastor at a church preached a fire and brimstone message (we don't hear this too often) about how hell has enlarged itself. The pastor related: "Hell has enlarged itself because it's getting some church folks there – some choir members, ushers, Sunday school teachers, superintendents, etc." Then the pastor paused as he exhaled, "and even some preachers and pastors": "Therefore hell hath enlarged herself, and opened her mouth without measure: and their glory, and their multitude, and their pomp, and he that rejoiceth, shall descend into it" (Isaiah 5:14). When one has sung their last song, prayed their last prayer, and gave their last testimony, they will stand before the Lord to hear either: "His lord said unto him, Well done, good and faithful servant; thou hast been faithful over a few things, I will make thee ruler over many things: enter thou into the joy of thy lord" (Matthew 25:23), or "And then will I profess unto them, I never knew you: depart from me, ye that work iniquity" (Matthew 7:23). "Then shall he say also unto them on the left hand, Depart from me, ye cursed, into everlasting fire, prepared for the devil and his angels" (Matthew 25:41). The woman in the Bible lost a coin so she lit a candle, swept the floor, and sought diligently to seek the coin until she found it (see Luke 15:8). Therefore, in truth and reality, one's sermon can exemplify a person who can be working in ministries and still be lost in the House of God.

I was at a large church one Sunday morning and the pastor had a visiting evangelist bring the message. This person never once opened the Bible to read. After a small talk, the congregation was asked to bring $100, 75, 50; or whatever amount you have to the altar. Afterward, the evangelist stated: "I don't make altar calls; I let the pastor do that." The pastor came up, gave a few words, and no altar call was made for sinners, no special prayer, nor was the doors opened for new members. Is this "the new wave ministry?" Imagine that after the benediction at the Sunday morning service, probably, just probably all in their circle went to dinner and each had a $100.00 plus meal, when souls were probably crying out for the altar call. Oh, it will be awesome to see more pastors called by God, who have a heart for all people and ministry. Therefore, this author is often reminded of "called pastors" from the Biblical passage of Jeremiah 3:15.

The spiritual side of the church will seek the will and guidance of the Lord Jesus Christ. "It's not about you, It's not about you – It's about the Lord!" When Jesus' parents realized their son was missing, and they found Him in the temple, Mary began to express words of concern: "And when they saw him, they were amazed: and his mother said unto him, Son, why hast thou thus dealt with us? behold, thy father and I have sought thee sorrowing" (Luke 2:48). Jesus responded to his parents in a spiritual encounter with two questions: "And he said unto them, How is it that ye sought me? wist ye not that I must be about my Father's business" (verse 49)? After these words, Jesus' parents did not understand their son's spiritual encounter or questions: "And they understood not the saying which he spake unto them" (verse 50). From childhood to adulthood, Jesus let nothing detour Him from his mission: "For I came down from heaven, not to do mine own will, but the will of him that sent me" (John 6:38).

On the earthly side of ministry, some leaders in the Body of Christ will start ministry doing the will of Jesus, and as time passes, they wear a different set of lenses which sees people as dollar signs, and they abuse their power in the gospel. The Apostle Paul speaks about leaders in ministry and the stewardship that is entrusted to them as they take heed to Biblical principles: "For though I preach the gospel, I have nothing to glory of: for necessity is laid upon me; yea, woe is unto me, if I preach not the gospel! For if I do this thing willingly, I have a reward: but if against my will, a dispensation of the gospel is committed unto me. What is my reward then? Verily that, when I preach the gospel, I may make the gospel of Christ without charge, that I abuse not my power in the gospel" (1 Corinthians 9:16-18).

They built their own house, and Jesus knocks on the door saying: "Let Me in." The response comes back with: "No, no, no." Jesus says: "I'll huff and puff and blow your house (ministry) down." Jesus blows their house down. They run and start building another ministry. Again, Jesus knocks on the door saying: "Let Me in." A response comes back with: "No, no, no." Jesus says: I'll huff and puff and blow your house down." Again, they run; but this time, they

I Woke Up One Day & Decided to LIVE!

build God's house on a solid rock, with Biblical principles because God spoke spiritual things into their life, and they took heed. Thereupon, they embrace all people, seeking Biblical principles, and wise counsel for God's direction and His favor.

A time in King Solomon's life when he sought the face of God, he called for a prayer meeting. This king made his own altar, reflected on the omnipresence (ever-presentness) of God, prayed for the people with a humble spirit in kneeling before them in prayer, and a spiritual unison erupted: "And he stood before the altar of the LORD in the presence of all the congregation of Israel, and spread forth his hands: For Solomon had made a brasen scaffold, of five cubits long, and five cubits broad, and three cubits high, and had set it in the midst of the court: and upon it he stood, and kneeled down upon his knees before all the congregation of Israel, and spread forth his hands toward heaven, And said, O LORD God of Israel, there is no God like thee in the heaven, nor in the earth; which keepest covenant, and shewest mercy unto thy servants, that walk before thee with all their hearts: Thou which hast kept with thy servant David my father that which thou hast promised him; and spakest with thy mouth, and hast fulfilled it with thine hand, as it is this day" (2 Chronicles 6:12-15).

King Solomon set an example in being a spiritual leader and seeking the Lord's **face** (His will, spiritual encounters) and guidance, not his **hand** (gimme, gimme, gimme; do, do, do). After the prayer of King Solomon, the glory of the Lord appeared: "NOW when Solomon had made an end of praying, the fire came down from heaven, and consumed the burnt offering and the sacrifices; and the glory of the LORD filled the house. And the priests could not enter into the house of the LORD, because the glory of the LORD had filled the LORD's house" (2 Chronicles 7:1, 2). When the household of faith begins to see the power of prayer and the Lord's manifestation, then, just maybe, many will return to church and see the old path in seeking the Lord's face and not his hand: "And when all the children of Israel saw how the fire came down, and the glory of the LORD upon the house, they bowed themselves with their faces to the ground upon the pavement, and worshipped, and praised the LORD, saying, For he is good; for his mercy endureth for ever" (verse 3).

The Finale – Being A Prayer Warrior!

Prayer is a powerful weapon that the Lord has given to the saints. Unfortunately, it is the least used weapon by some, who confess Jesus Christ as their Lord and Savior. Some Believers want to pray when trouble comes, but the Bible says: "that men ought always to pray, and not to faint" (Luke 18:1b). The power of prayer manifested itself when the saints gathered at Mary's house, in being of one accord to pray for Peter's release from prison. The saints knew they had to pray for Peter's release from prison, because Herod had already killed James, and Peter was next for execution: "And he killed James the brother of John with the sword" (Acts 12:2). Therefore, in coming together for prayer, and being of one accord - one does not pray about having a spouse and others pray about a financial breakthrough. The saints came together to pray for Peter's release from prison. While they prayed in one accord, a knock came at the door and Rhoda, a damsel, quietly removed herself from prayer to answer the knock. She saw Peter, and was shocked, and left him standing at the door: "And as Peter knocked at the door of the gate, a damsel came to hearken, named Rhoda" (verse 13). Afterward, she hurriedly interrupted the saints' prayer and said that Peter was at the door of the gate! They perhaps thought she was delusional because they said: "Thou art mad" (verse 15a). The young girl, Rhoda, tried to convince them, but they likely thought, that since they were in prayer, she saw a vision and affirmed her: "It is his angel" (verse 15b). Between them trying to convince her and her telling them who she saw, Peter kept knocking: "But Peter continued knocking: and when they had opened the door, and saw him, they were astonished" (verse 16). The saints will often say: "The Lord will answer you while you're calling Him."

I believe prisoners being released from incarceration can bring about social change in the church. It appears that some pastors and leaders in the church have allowed Satan and his angels to use them as participants in trying to destroy the church in their own ungodly ways. Therefore, the Body of Christ needs to "pray" and not "prey." The Revelation of the Church entails: "And I say also unto thee, That thou art Peter, and upon this rock I will build my church; and the gates of hell shall not prevail against it. And I will give unto thee the keys of the kingdom of heaven: and whatsoever thou shalt bind on earth shall be bound in heaven: and whatsoever thou shalt loose on earth shall be loosed in heaven. Then charged he his disciples that they should tell no man that he was Jesus the Christ" (Matthew 16:18-20).

Moral – Biblical and Life-Living:
I cannot continue to sit here and be isolated from loved ones, when my destiny unfolds itself – I must bring about social change

---

Incarcerated Prisoners, A Person that Allows Their Destiny to Unfold

Discussion Questions

Do you see the association of "men with leprosy" being isolated from their family and community and "incarcerated prisoners" being isolated? If you do not see any difference, please discuss it.

With your spiritual lens, does it appear that Satan and his angels are using God's own people as participants in trying to destroy the church in being more "commercial" than "spiritual?" If so, please discuss your insight. If not, please share.

What are some ways your ministry can bring about "social change" in the church and community?

Think about Walter Hawkins Love Alive Choir 3 singing, *Don't Wait till the Battle is over shout now.* Tell us, "How do you give God the praise in the midst of your calamity?"

It appears that when some people are in confinement, they will indulge themselves with the things of the Lord, and when their deliverance comes, the Lord is put on the back burner. Why do you believe this behavior manifests itself?

How do you glorify the Lord in the midst of "going through" your trials and tribulations? One preacher said: "Ask God what He is telling you in the midst of. . ."

Have you ever prayed about something and God answered you while calling Him?

Case Study:
Pastor Brighton has called a prayer meeting for one hour at the church on Wednesdays at 7:00 pm for two weeks - One hour of

prayer: "And he cometh unto the disciples, and findeth them asleep, and saith unto Peter, What, could ye not watch with me one hour" (Matthew 26:40)? This prayer meeting is to pray for God's guidance on how to win souls into the Body of Christ. The pastor believes the Lord has given him this call for a prayer meeting at the church. The Church Mother, Tolado says that some people do not have transportation to make it to prayer. Therefore, she suggests to the pastor that people call each other on the phone for God's guidance on how to win souls into the Body of Christ. The pastor believes the prayer meeting is of the Lord and is to take place at the church. The church mother strongly believes that some people will not attend because of transportation, and the pastor should consider her suggestion. In the two giving their beliefs to the congregation, the majority of saints concur with the church mother. The pastor closes the meeting by inviting those who will, to be at the church for prayer on Wednesdays at 7:00 pm for two weeks, and for one hour of prayer. Afterward, the church mother gives the pastor a stern look.

Prayerful Reflection

Dear Father,
Thank You for helping us to realize that with You in our lives we are never alone. Isolation comes in so many forms. As we look at the various distractions from the truth of Your Word, we see those who are focused on collecting money, instead of reaching those who are outcast like the ten lepers, or riddled with guilt from past failures, like the incarcerated.

We cry, "Mercy Lord!" We already know how unclean our lives are. But we long for and desperately need Your mercy. Wash us of our unclean behaviors and thoughts so that we might be able to serve You with thankful hearts.

Elijah, A Prophet of God in Contest With the Prophets of Baal

From Death Wish to Chariot of Fire

"But he himself went a day's journey into the wilderness, and came and sat down under a juniper tree: and he requested for himself that he might die; and said, It is enough; now, O LORD, take away my life; for I am not better than my fathers."

1 Kings 19:4

"And it came to pass, as they still went on, and talked, that, behold, there appeared a chariot of fire, and horses of fire, and parted them both asunder; and Elijah went up by a whirlwind into heaven."

2 Kings 2:11

The name Elijah means "Yahweh is God." This prophet spoke miracles to happen, prophesied against King Ahab, asked a widow for a morsel of bread, stretched out and cried out to God for the resurrection of a woman's son, and he called a contest on Mt. Carmel with the prophets of Baal. This man of God was used in the spiritual realm, and he launched out into the prophetic and spiritual realms. In spite of his spiritual encounters with God, a spirit of depression took hold of prophet Elijah, until he himself sat under a juniper tree and requested of the Lord to die – All because of this one woman, "Jezebel," and her threat.

Clark (1980) awesome book, *God's Remedy for Depression*, is written from a Biblical perspective, reveals Biblical persons being depressed, and then shows God's remedy for their depression. In the midst of her writing this book, she was contemplating suicide and asked: "What was the point in continuing to live" (p. 9)? In the midst of her contemplating suicide, the Lord called her name and spoke a Rhema word to her: "Vivian, I'm not finished with you yet... besides, you're not finished with that book" (p. 9).

Martin (2002), a medical doctor, prophetically states in her book, *Saving Our Last Nerve: The Black Woman's Path to Mental Health*, "the mindset" of some leaders in the church regarding mental illness versus medical illness:

"Some church leaders have even encouraged their members to avoid psychiatric medications and treatment. I find it interesting that if a church member has been seriously ill with a physical condition, recovers and returns to the church, the minister and the congregation publicly praise her. But if a church member is stricken by severe depression and eventually recovers, her welcome back isn't nearly as openly celebrated. So we see that both the mental health and faith communities have often neglected what is best for the individual-a holistic approach to care" (p. 171).

"In 2008, Congress passed the Paul Wellstone and Peter Domenici Mental Health Parity and Addiction Equity Act (MHPAEA) to ensure equal coverage of treatment for mental illness and addiction. In November 2013, the federal government released rules to implement the law. Before this law, mental health treatment was typically covered at far lower levels in health insurance policies than physical illness" (http://www.nami.org).

According to the DSM-5 (2013), mental disorder is defined as:
"A mental disorder is a syndrome characterized by a clinically significant disturbance in an individual's cognition, emotion regulation, or behavior that reflects a dysfunction in the psychological,

biological, or developmental processes underlying mental functioning. Mental disorders are usually associated with significant distress or disability in social, occupation, or other important activities. An expectable or culturally approved response to a common stressor or loss, such as the death of a loved one, is not a mental disorder. Socially deviant behavior (e.g., political, religious, or sexual) and conflicts that are primarily between the individual and society are not mental disorders unless the deviance or conflict results from a dysfunction in the individual . . ." (p. 20).

The medical field and the federal law avail themselves of a different set of lenses regarding mental health and addiction; the DSM-5, also helps one's understanding of "mental disorder." Dr. Marilyn Martin through the lens of some church leaders "mindset" regarding mental illness, the federal law lens incorporated into law as "parity" (equal) "treatment for mental illness and addiction," and the DSM-5 lens also gives the definition of "mental disorder." Therefore, it is with sadness that some leaders and some people in the Body of Christ will have the audacity to say to people who are depressed, diagnosed with a mental illness, and/or have an addiction: "Saints shouldn't get depressed, you need to believe God (and you do), you don't believe God enough, bind that spirit of depression, Satan take your hands off the mind, you can't have it, shake it off, that ain't nothing but the work of the enemy, loose here in the name of Jesus, just because your daddy was a drunk; you don't have to be one, etc." Being in the spiritual realm is an awesome place to be. While at the same time, one cannot be so "heavenly minded and no earthly good."

To help alleviate some of these sayings, the saints will often say in their testimony: "I thank the Lord for being clothed and in my right mind:" This saying seems to present itself from the scripture: "And they come to Jesus, and see him that was possessed with the devil, and had the legion, sitting, and clothed, and in his right mind: and they were afraid" (Mark 5:15). I was at a church service one Sunday morning and the pastor who was very engaging and exemplifies much love and concern for all people arose to the sacred podium to preach the Word. As he looked over the congregation with a smile, as much as his medical sickness would allow him, he stated: "Ya'll don't need to go see no psychiatrist, psychologist, counselor, nor mental health people because they will mess your mind up." Oh, how some in the congregation responded with amen, hallelujah, hands waved, and colorful handkerchiefs waved in the air, even some head nods. What tended to raise an eyebrow with me was, the pastor receiving medical treatment to stay alive, while professionals in the mental health field can help one to keep their mind, stay sane, and not go off on folks (including some church folks). In truth with some people in the Body of Christ, a medical diagnosis tends to be more accepted versus a mental diagnosis. One needs to be just as smart about mental health as medical health – they both are equally important. My former professor said in class: "If anything has to go with me, don't let it be my mind." A family therapist would say regarding diagnosis: "one voice among many."

Another time, I was at a revival service and the Lord used the evangelist in a prophetic way, as the people lined up. The evangelist reminds one of Isaiah, the prophet, who saw things in the spirit and spoke "what thus saith the Lord." One lady at the end of the line appeared to be sad and depressed. The evangelist spoke prophetic words to her that she did not refute. The evangelist anointed, prayed and prayed for the lady, and to no avail, her countenance did not change; nor was she delivered from her trouble(s). He called for prayer warriors to pray for her, and the same prevailed. The lady left the altar still appearing to look sad and depressed. Afterward, I wanted to give her my card and say: "I am a licensed professional counselor. Please come and see me for psychotherapy. If you don't have the money, I will do a session pro bono - free."

Elijah, A Prophet of God Being in Contest with the Prophets of Baal

After standing firm and calling on the name of God in a contest on Mount Carmel (which God won), the prophet Elijah received a death threat from Jezebel: "Then Jezebel sent a messenger unto Elijah, saying, So let the gods do to me, and more also, if I make not thy life as the life of one of them by to morrow about this time" (1 Kings 19:2). This death threat caused the prophet Elijah to flee from Jezebel, sit under a juniper tree, and request of God to die (a death wish): "But he himself went a day's journey into the wilderness, and came and sat down under a juniper tree: and he requested for himself that he might die; and said, It is enough; now, O LORD, take away my life; for I am not better than my fathers" (verse 4). Some people (including Christians) cannot fathom Elijah requesting death after his spiritual encounter on Mount Carmel. Therefore, one must be mindful of the Scripture: "if it were possible, they shall deceive the very elect" (Matthew 24:24b). In the midst of Elijah being focused on his depression, Jezebel's death threat, rejections, and being all alone in the battle; he thought when God spoke to him, He was in the wind, earthquake, and fire, but God was in a "still small voice" as He asked him a question, and called him by his name: "What doest thou here, Elijah" (1 Kings 19:9b, 13b)? A "still small voice" can be a song, a scripture, a word you heard along the way, one's physical presence, or other spiritual encounters.

There was a time in my life when I was so despondent with the cares and needs in my life. I felt like the prophet Elijah – Lord it is enough, take away my life (see 1 Kings 19:4). While focusing on my troubles, uncontrollable tears began to flow while driving; until I had to pull over. I could not stop the uncontrollable tears from coming. In the midst of my tears, a "still small voice" came to me with the words: *"It won't be like this always."* Immediately, I dried my tears and said: "Lord, I believe that is a song." I searched the words on YouTube, and up came the late Rev. Timothy Wright's song – *It*

I Woke Up One Day & Decided to LIVE!

Won't Be This Way Always. Rev. Wright and LaShun Pace were singing many words in the song that reflected what I was going through. In a prelude to him singing *Who's On The Lord's Side*, the late Rev. Timothy Wright stated: "I asked God to give me songs that will encourage the saints." The Lord has done just that and manifested Himself. In the movie, *Color Purple*, when Sofia, was in a bad place in her life, eventually going to work for the Mayor's wife, she ran into Miss Celie at the grocery store. During this misfortunate dilemma in her life, Miss Celie's presence was a "still small voice" to her. Later at the dinner table, Sofia reminisced on that day (hilarious): "Sat in that jail, I sat in that jail til I near about done rot to death. I know what it like to wanna go somewhere and cain't. I know what it like to wanna sing... and have it beat out 'ya. I want to thank you, Miss Celie, for everything you done for me. I 'members that day in the store with Miss Millie - I's feelin' real down. I's feelin' mighty bad. And when I see'd you - I know'd there is a God. I know'd there is a God. And one day I was gonna get to come home" (http://www.imdb.com/title/tt0088939/quotes). A "still small voice" can carry one over in knowing "There is a God" who cares about His people, and makes intercession for them in the midst of decisions and turmoil. I heard one preacher say in his sermon: "Sometimes your situation may not change, but just to hear a word from the Lord will make everything alright."

Believers of Jesus Christ often reiterate to themselves and others: "It ain't over, till God says it's over." It was not over with the prophet Elijah. The Lord will not leave His own people to wallow down and perish in the midst of depression and oppression. Therefore, life was spoken into the prophet, as he picked up the torch and began to speak into the lives of other leaders, and to continue in the prophetic ministry: "Go... anoint Hazael to be king over Syria... Jehu... anoint to be king over Israel: and Elisha... shalt thou anoint to be prophet in thy room" (1 Kings 19:15, 16). Elijah continued to launch out as he spoke prophetic words to his enemy, King Ahab, regarding him and his wife, Jezebel's death: "And of Jezebel also spake the LORD, saying, The dogs shall eat Jezebel by the wall of Jezreel. Him that dieth of Ahab in the city the dogs shall eat; and him that dieth in the field shall the fowls of the air eat. But there was none like unto Ahab, which did sell himself to work wickedness in the sight of the LORD, whom Jezebel his wife stirred up. And he did very abominably in following idols, according to all things as did the Amorites, whom the LORD cast out before the children of Israel" (1 Kings 21:23-26). After the prophetic words, King Ahab repented and humbled himself: "And it came to pass, when Ahab heard those words, that he rent his clothes, and put sackcloth upon his flesh, and fasted, and lay in sackcloth, and went softly" (verse 27).

Because of King Ahab's humility, God did not bring evil to him, but in his son's days and upon his son's house: "Seest thou how Ahab humbleth himself before me? because he humbleth himself before me, I will not bring the evil in his days: but in his son's days will I bring the evil upon his house" (1 Kings 21:29). This spirit of humility, humbleness reminds one of the prophetic words from the prophet Isaiah to King Hezekiah: "IN those days was Hezekiah sick unto death. And the prophet Isaiah the son of Amoz came to him, and said unto him, Thus saith the LORD, Set thine house in order; for thou shalt die, and not live. Then he turned his face to the wall, and prayed unto the LORD, saying, I beseech thee, O LORD, remember now how I have walked before thee in truth and with a perfect heart, and have done that which is good in thy sight. And Hezekiah wept sore" (2 Kings 20:1-3). This spirit of repentance caused a miraculous recovery, where the Lord spoke to Isaiah in the middle of the court with a "changed mind": "Turn again, and tell Hezekiah the captain of my people, Thus saith the LORD, the God of David thy father, I have heard thy prayer, I have seen thy tears: behold, I will heal thee: on the third day thou shalt go up unto the house of the LORD. And I will add unto thy days fifteen years; and I will deliver thee and this city out of the hand of the king of Assyria; and I will defend this city for mine own sake, and for my servant David's sake" (verses 5, 6).

The prophet Elijah requested to die under a juniper tree, but God saw differently: "And it came to pass, as they still went on, and talked, that, behold, there appeared a chariot of fire, and horses of fire, and parted them both asunder; and Elijah went up by a whirlwind into heaven" (2 Kings 2:11). Prior to this encounter, Elisha followed Elijah to Bethel, Jericho, and Jordan. Each time, Elijah told Elisha to wait, while he went on his journey: "Tarry here, I pray thee; for the LORD hath sent me to Bethel" (verse 2a), "tarry here, I pray thee; for the LORD hath sent me to Jericho" (verse 4a), "Tarry, I pray thee, here; for the LORD hath sent me to Jordan" (verse 6a). Each time, Elisha responded with: "I will not leave thee" (verses 2, 4, 6). More often than not, some leaders do not want to follow the senior leaders God has assigned to them. They will not allow leaders to speak into their life and give them wise counsel. Therefore Biblical principles may apply: "The way of a fool is right in his own eyes: but he that hearkeneth unto counsel is wise" (Proverbs 12:15).

Many years ago, I was at a church meeting, and the bishop sat patiently in the pulpit, as he periodically glanced over the congregation and listened to different pastors give honor to God and recognition to the bishop and others. Afterward, the bishop rose from his comfortable chair, stepped to the sacred podium with both hands on the edge of the sacred podium. No words came from the bishop's mouth. A few seconds later, he stepped from the sacred podium to the edge of the pulpit, and flipped the script in the household of faith by saying (with that Celie hand up to Mister from the *Color Purple* movie): "Everything you done to me, already done to you." The church was quiet, where one could hear a pin drop. I said to myself: "Maybe, just maybe some pastors did not make their report, and/or they did not do what the bishop asked them to do." If the truth presents itself, pastors ask their members to do similar things that the bishop asked the pastors to do, and to no avail was it reciprocated to the bishop from some pastors.

In following with prophet Elijah, the sons of the prophets tried to deter Elisha saying: "Knowest thou that the LORD will take away thy master from thy head to day? (2 Kings 2:3b, 5b). Each time Elisha came back with: "Yea, I know it; hold ye your peace (verses 3c, 5c). In the midst of prophet Elijah asking him to wait for him and the sons of the prophets telling him his master will be taken away, Elisha was persistent to his call to follow the man of God and to receive his blessing in being obedient. In the end, the prophet Elijah asked him a question, and Elisha answered with a surety: "And it came to pass, when they were gone over, that Elijah said unto Elisha, Ask what I shall do for thee, before I be taken away from thee. And Elisha said, I pray thee, let a double portion of thy spirit be upon me" (verse 9). Prophet Elijah's response came back with reality, maybe due to his own rejections and loneliness that he encountered during his ministry: "And he said, Thou hast asked a hard thing: nevertheless, if thou see me when I am taken from thee, it shall be so unto thee; but if not, it shall not be so" (verse 10). In order to receive the blessing, Elisha had to stay with the leader. This is a lesson within itself for leaders. If only more leaders will follow Godly leaders, what unity it will be in the Body of Christ. As a child, we would often play the game: "Follow the Leader." I remember very distinctly marching behind the leader, even when the leader took us in circles.

I Woke Up One Day & Decided to LIVE!

From a Biblical perspective, there were times God spoke to leaders for their deliverance, which just doesn't add up in the human's finite mind.

Moses, the leader, had the children of Israel walk into the midst of the Red Sea, after the waters were divided: "And Moses stretched out his hand over the sea; and the LORD caused the sea to go back by a strong east wind all that night, and made the sea dry land, and the waters were divided. And the children of Israel went into the midst of the sea upon the dry ground: and the waters were a wall unto them on their right hand, and on their left" (Exodus 14:21, 22). The children of Israel had the Red Sea in front of them and Pharaoh and his army behind them. In Israel's anguish, they reminded Moses about what they told him in Egypt – leave us alone, and let us stay in Egypt: "Is not this the word that we did tell thee in Egypt, saying, Let us alone, that we may serve the Egyptians? For it had been better for us to serve the Egyptians, than that we should die in the wilderness" (verse 12). Moses tried to console the people's fear, and keep them focused. But they would not hear tell-of-such. God is a man of His word: "God is not a man, that he should lie; neither the son of man, that he should repent: hath he said, and shall he not do it? or hath he spoken, and shall he not make it good" (Numbers 23:19)? It has often been said, "If God said it, I believe it, and that settles that!" God told Moses He was going to deliver His people, Israel out of Egypt, so that they may serve Him; therefore, there was no turning back in the face of their opposition with Pharaoh and his company. After God delivered the children of Israel out of Egypt, we read throughout the Bible that, He brought the children of Israel out of Egypt with a mighty strong hand.

It has been said that Egypt represents "bondage": "I am the LORD thy God, which have brought thee out of the land of Egypt, out of the house of bondage" (Exodus 20:2). When some Believers are in a bad situation(s), their prayer is: "Lord, get me out of Egypt." Jacob (Israel) lived in Egypt seventeen years, and when the time came for his death, he specifically told his son, Joseph, to get him out of Egypt and not to bury his bones in Egypt: "But I will lie with my fathers, and thou shalt carry me out of Egypt, and bury me in their buryingplace. And he said, I will do as thou hast said" (Genesis 47:30). Jacob was so serious about his burial place and his bones not being in Egypt that he asked his son to make him a promise: "And he said, Swear unto me, And he sware unto him. And Israel bowed himself upon the bed's head" (verse 31). Joseph upheld his promise: "My father made me swear, saying, Lo, I die: in my grave which I have digged for me in the land of Canaan, there shalt thou bury me. Now therefore let me go up, I pray thee, and bury my father, and I will come again" (Genesis 50:5). The time near Joseph's death, he too did not want his bones in Egypt: "ye shall carry up my bones from hence" (Genesis 50:25b). It was Moses who took the bones of Joseph out of Egypt: "And Moses took the bones of Joseph with him: for he had straitly sworn the children of Israel, saying, God will surely visit you; and ye shall carry up my bones away hence with you" (Exodus 13:19).

Moses was in the middle of a rock and hard place with the heavy load of the people; being blamed for delivering Israel from captivity and bondage from the hands of Pharaoh and his taskmasters. The Lord spoke to Moses with a question, gave him "marching orders" for Israel, and told him to use **his rod – the rod used previously to work miracles** - the rod that was in Moses' hand from the Mountain of Horeb – the Mountain of God, when God spoke to him about returning to Egypt to deliver his people, Israel:

> "And thou shalt take this rod in thine hand, wherewith thou shalt do signs" (Exodus 4:17), Aaron's rod that swallowed Pharaoh's rod: "And Moses and Aaron went in unto Pharaoh,

and they did so as the LORD had commanded: and Aaron cast down his rod before Pharaoh, and before his servants, and it became a serpent" (Exodus 7:10); and the rod he used for the plague to turn the Nile River into blood: "And the LORD spake unto Moses, Say unto Aaron, Take thy rod, and stretch out thine hand upon the waters of Egypt, upon their streams, upon their rivers, and upon their ponds, and upon all their pools of water, that they may become blood; and that there may be blood throughout all the land of Egypt, both in vessels of wood, and in vessels of stone" (Exodus 7:19).

In the midst of Israel's distress with their opponents, the Lord came in a cool, calm, and collective manner: "And the LORD said unto Moses, Wherefore criest thou unto me? speak unto the children of Israel, that they go forward: But lift thou up thy rod, and stretch out thine hand over the sea, and divide it: and the children of Israel shall go on dry ground through the midst of the sea" (Exodus 14:15, 16).

Joshua, the leader, Moses' successor had the people walk around the city, with armed men. Specific instructions were given for victory at Jericho: get up early every morning, walk around the city six times, seven priests bear before the ark seven trumpets of rams' horns, wait for the long blast, the sound of the trumpet, and do not open up your mouth to speak; until I, Joshua tell you to "shout": "And the LORD said unto Joshua, See, I have given into thine hand Jericho, and the king thereof, and the mighty men of valour. And ye shall compass the city, all ye men of war, and go round about the city once. Thus shalt thou do six days. And seven priests shall bear before the ark seven trumpets of rams' horns: and the seventh day ye shall compass the city seven times, and the priests shall blow with the trumpets" (Joshua 6:2-4). The seventh day: "And it came to pass on the seventh day, that they rose early about the dawning of the day, and compassed the city after the same manner seven times: only on that day they compassed the city seven times" (verse 15). In taking heed to Joshua, the leader, the finale for victory manifested itself: "So the people shouted when the priests blew with the trumpets: and it came to pass, when the people heard the sound of the trumpet, and the people shouted with a great shout, that the wall fell down flat, so that the people went up into the city, every man straight before him, and they took the city" (verse 20). There is a city that often speaks about taking their city back. This sounds great! While at the same time: "How can you take the city back, when there are too many chiefs and not enough Indians?"

King Jehoshaphat appointed singers to praise the Lord for their deliverance. The king admitted his fear with his enemies. "And Jehoshaphat feared, and set himself to seek the LORD, and proclaimed a fast throughout all Judah. And Judah gathered themselves together, to ask help of the LORD: even out of all the cities of Judah they came to seek the LORD" (2 Chronicles 20:3, 4). Judah means "Let God be praised," and God's people upheld the meaning in singing praises for their deliverance. The Lord guided and assured them: "Ye shall not need to fight in this battle: set yourselves, stand ye still, and see the salvation of the LORD with you, O Judah and Jerusalem: fear not, nor be dismayed; to morrow go out against them: for the LORD will be with you" (verse 17). The saints will say, "Set yourself."

The battle was fought with "appointed singers": "And when he had consulted with the people, he appointed singers unto the LORD, and that should praise the beauty of holiness, as they went out before the army, and to say, Praise the LORD; for his mercy endureth for ever" (2 Chronicles 20:21). The Lord set up ambushments (strategies concealment for surprise attacks), where Judah's enemies turned on their own people. "And when they began to sing and to praise, the LORD set ambushments against the children of Ammon, Moab, and mount Seir, which were come against Judah; and they were smitten. For the children of Ammon and Moab stood up against the inhabitants of mount Seir, utterly to slay and destroy them: and when they had made an end of the inhabitants of Seir, every one helped to destroy another" (verses 22, 23). A surprise attack reminds this author of the *Gomer Pyle* show, when Sergeant Carter would try to get information out of Private *Gomer Pyle* and he would look at his Sergeant with a big smile, turning his head from side to side, saying: "Surprise, Surprise, Surprise." The sergeant became so frustrated because he could not get any information out of one of his own troops. Some would say, Gomer is "insubordinate to his superior."

In taking wise counsel from King Jehoshaphat, the people ended up with the spoil (leftover) from the deceased: "And when Jehoshaphat and his people came to take away the spoil of them, they found among them in abundance both riches with the dead bodies, and precious jewels, which they stripped off for themselves, more than they could carry away: and they were three days in gathering of the spoil, it was so much" (2 Chronicles 20:25). The Bible says: "the wealth of the sinner is laid up for the just" (Proverbs 13:22b).

The late Rev. James Cleveland gave a sermonette "How We Praise God" from a recording of "Down Memory Lane" (1973) about following instructions. He gives a scenario using instructions in baking a cake. He wanted a cake, so he went to the store to purchase one. Upon his return home, he made the cake, and it did not turn out right. So he made another trip to the store. This time, he read the instructions on the back of the box for baking a cake. He incorporated this learned experience in orchestrating the musicians to play their musical instruments separately – the tambourine, drum, string instruments, and lastly, everything that hath breath: "Praise him with the sound of the trumpet: praise him with the psaltery and harp. Praise him with the timbrel and dance: praise him with stringed instruments and organs. Praise him upon the loud cymbals: praise him upon the high sounding cymbals. Let every thing that hath breath praise the LORD. Praise ye the LORD" (Psalm 150:3-6). The late Rev. James Cleveland gives the instructions for the church: "If you want to have church, for the best results, you need to follow the directions." Therefore, we need spiritual leaders that will hear from the Lord, and speak what thus saith the Lord to the Body of Christ.

It is unfortunate that some leaders will not follow directions nor stay with the leader. They may feel they are more theologically based, educated, more anointed, prophetically sound, have longevity in the field of ministry, or other unforeseen situations. Some will even adopt some of the young folk's language: "I got this." If one is not careful in following good leadership, they can fall into the snares of the enemy, and it can be like Joe Tex's song, *I Gotcha*. Yea, Joe Tex is singing about a broken relationship, with a promise to another. But the snares of the enemy can catch one unaware, when they're not covered under good leadership guidance. Elisha stayed with the leader, Elijah, and in the end, he witnessed a chariot of fire taking the prophet Elijah: "And it came to pass, as they still went on, and talked, that, behold, there appeared a chariot of fire, and horses of fire, and parted them both asunder; and Elijah went up by a whirlwind into heaven" (2 Kings 2:11). Elisha witnessed an anointed prophet being taken away: "And Elisha saw it, and he cried, My father, my father, the chariot of Israel, and the horsemen thereof. And he saw him no more: and he took hold of his own clothes, and rent them in two pieces" (verse 12).

The prophet Elijah did not die under the juniper tree. **He Woke Up and Decided to Live when he took heed to the "still small voice"**

from God, began to speak into the lives of other leaders, continued his prophetic ministry, and confronted his enemy, King Ahab. The prophet's life on earth ended in being taken by a chariot of fire. Afterward, Elisha took Elijah's mantle and received a double portion of the prophet's spirit. After Elisha's death, while in his grave, a dead man's body touched the bones of Elisha, and the dead man revived: "And it came to pass, as they were burying a man, that, behold, they spied a band of men; and they cast the man into the sepulchre of Elisha: and when the man was let down, and touched the bones of Elisha, he revived, and stood up on his feet" (2 Kings 13:21). The spirit of Elisha, who followed the leader to the end, received a double portion of the prophet Elijah's spirit.

Moral – Biblical and Life-Living:
A spirit of depression sat under the juniper tree, spoke death – But a "still small voice" speaks life into the leadership in me

---

Discussion Questions

Elijah, the prophet, was not suicidal. He appears to be depressed. There are people who are depressed and see no purpose or meaning in living, may feel (unfortunately) that their only option is suicide. If a person is contemplating suicide or in a crisis, who can they call? (The secular world has something in place for suicide – 1 (800) 273-8255 National Suicide Prevention Lifeline www.suicidepreventionlifeline.org). The pastor cannot do it all! Moses tried, until his father-in-law, Jethro, pulled him aside with wise counsel that the people would wear him out, and for Moses to raise up leaders to handle small things and for him to handle the big things (see Exodus 18: 14-24). In establishing or already have a counseling ministry, please do not have people on the ministry team who are critical, judgmental, biased, work in partiality, gossip; nor

Elijah, A Prophet of God Being in Contest with the Prophets of Baal

ones that will throw the Bible at people in putting them on a guilt trip. (wise counsel from this author).

Are there any telltale signs of a suicidal person?

What is a crisis?
Are crisis interventions a part of new membership class, and is it periodically mentioned in the bulletin as to its availability to the Body of Christ and community?

To be a leader, one must have followers. If not, you are just taking a walk. Why is it that some leaders will not follow other leaders in authority?

In some churches when the doors of the church are opened, they say: "Come by letter or by experience." When leaders in ministry come for membership from another church, should they come by letter or by experience to continue in a leadership position?

Elisha followed Elijah all the way until he received a "double portion" of Elijah's spirit. In the interim in following Elijah to different places, they talked. Why is it difficult for some potential leaders to walk alongside the leader, take wise counsel, listen, and take heed? There is an old saying: "Boy, you need to sit down and hear somebody."

In the spiritual arena, when you hear a voice, how do you know it is the Lord's "still small voice?"

Case Study:
Marlee is a single mother of three small children (ages 3, 4, 7). She has been a member of the church for two years. Marlee is a reserved person, where she basically keeps to herself. For some reason or

another, she befriends you and tells you she has attempted suicide three times in her life, and that she struggles with this. She also confessed being a born again believer of Jesus Christ. Because of the troubles in her life, she says: "I don't care if I wake up in the morning."

Assess Your Biblical Knowledge On Mental Illness
(http://www.bible.ca):

A. The cases of insanity in the Bible:
1. **Balaam** wanted to curse Israel for money even though forbidden by God: "forsaking the right way, they have gone astray, having followed the way of Balaam, the son of Beor, who loved the wages of unrighteousness; but he received a rebuke for his own transgression, for a mute donkey, speaking with a voice of a man, restrained the madness of the prophet." (2 Peter 2:15-16)
2. **David** faked mental illness and was wrongly accused of being insane by the King of Gath: "David took these words to heart and greatly feared Achish king of Gath. So he disguised his sanity before them, and acted insanely in their hands, and scribbled on the doors of the gate, and let his saliva run down into his beard. Then Achish said to his servants, "Behold, you see the man behaving as a madman. Why do you bring him to me? "Do I lack madmen, that you have brought this one to act the madman in my presence? Shall this one come into my house?"" (1 Samuel 21:12-15)
3. **King Saul** who drove himself insane out of hatred for David and rebellion to God: "Now it came about on the next day that an evil spirit from God came mightily upon Saul, and he raved in the midst of the house, while David was

playing the harp with his hand, as usual; and a spear was in Saul's hand. Saul hurled the spear for he thought, "I will pin David to the wall." But David escaped from his presence twice. Now Saul was afraid of David, for the Lord was with him but had departed from Saul." (1 Samuel 18:10-12)

4. **Nebuchadnezzar** was stricken with dementia and loss of reason by God for his pride: "While the word was in the king's mouth, a voice came from heaven, saying, 'King Nebuchadnezzar, to you it is declared: sovereignty has been removed from you, and you will be driven away from mankind, and your dwelling place will be with the beasts of the field. You will be given grass to eat like cattle, and seven periods of time will pass over you until you recognize that the Most High is ruler over the realm of mankind and bestows it on whomever He wishes.' "Immediately the word concerning Nebuchadnezzar was fulfilled; and he was driven away from mankind and began eating grass like cattle, and his body was drenched with the dew of heaven until his hair had grown like eagles' feathers and his nails like birds' claws. "But at the end of that period, I, Nebuchadnezzar, raised my eyes toward heaven and my reason returned to me, and I blessed the Most High and praised and honored Him who lives forever; For His dominion is an everlasting dominion, And His kingdom endures from generation to generation." (Daniel 4:31–34)

5. **John the Baptist** was wrongly accused of being insane: "For John came neither eating nor drinking, and they say, 'He has a demon!'" (Matthew 11:18)

6. **Jesus** was wrongly accused of being insane: "Many of them were saying, "He has a demon and is insane. Why do you listen to Him?" Others were saying, "These are not the sayings of one demon-possessed. A demon cannot open

the eyes of the blind, can he?"" (John 10:20-21)
7. **Paul** was wrongly accused of being mad: "While Paul was saying this in his defense, Festus said in a loud voice, "Paul, you are out of your mind! Your great learning is driving you mad." (Acts 26:24)

B. The Bible's Mental illness checklist:
1. Willing to curse the very God who made you a prophet. (Balaam)
2. lack of proper judgment and discernment (David)
3. scribbled on the doors of the gate (David)
4. saliva run down into his beard (David)
5. Making ridiculous claims about yourself (Jesus was making a true statement they rejected)
6. Sinful behavior (Saul/Nebuchadnezzar)
7. rebellion and insubordination (Saul)
8. Will not accept the advice of others: uncounselable. (Saul/Nebuchadnezzar)
9. Irreconcilable. (Saul)
10. Lack of repentance when rebuked (Saul)
11. Self-righteousness and pride (Saul/Nebuchadnezzar)
12. Spiritual elitism (Saul/Nebuchadnezzar)
13. Intense jealousy and anger directed at an innocent person (Saul)
14. Fear and panic attacks (Saul)
15. suspicion and paranoia (Saul)
16. music/drugs don't help much (Saul)
17. Discounting personal responsibility (Saul)
18. Masters at hiding the real problem (Saul)
19. Talking about God, judgment and the afterlife (Jesus)
20. Dressing and eating foods outside the normal lifestyle choices (John the Baptist)
21. Manic, hyperness (Paul was excited and forceful in his

      teaching)
22. tunnel vision, excessive intensity on a single goal at the wrong time (Paul appeared to be consumed by the gospel)

Prayerful Reflection

Dear Father,
Thank You for the example of Elijah in Your Word, to remind us that even after great successes we can find ourselves in despair because of one minor threat. Help us to take care of ourselves in times of distress so that we can complete the journey before us with victory so that those who pick up the mantel after us may experience a double portion of Your power. Thank You for examples like Moses, Joshua, Hezekiah, and Saul so we can be mindful of our desperate need to praise You and trust You no matter how things look.

A Samaritan Woman

Her Testimony Changed a Community

"The woman then left her waterpot, and went her way into the city, and saith to the men, Come, see a man, which told me all things that ever I did: is not this the Christ? Then they went out of the city, and came unto him."

John 4:28-30

The Samaritans were of a mixed race and outcast by the Jews, and there was no value or communication between the two races. Therefore, when Jesus started talking to a Samaritan woman at Jacob's Well, this woman could not understand why Jesus would take time out to commune with her: "Then saith the woman of Samaria unto him, How is it that thou, being a Jew, askest drink of me, which am a woman of Samaria? for the Jews have no dealings with the Samaritans" (John 4:9). To answer her question and soothe her curiosity: "Jesus answered and said unto her, If thou knewest the gift of God, and who it is that saith to thee, Give me to drink; thou wouldest have asked of him, and he would have given thee living water" (verse 10). This man, Jesus who had needs to go through Samaria, where He met this woman that He knew would be alone at Jacob's Well: "And he must needs go through Samaria" (verse 4). His disciples were gone to the city to buy food, and it was the sixth hour of the day (noon).

Therefore in witnessing, one must be: "wise as serpents, and harmless as doves" (Matthew 10:16b). In working miracles, one has to put out unbelieving people because they will not have any hope for people, will cast them out, and be ready to call the undertaker for burial: "He said unto them, Give place: for the maid is not dead, but sleepeth. And they laughed him to scorn. But when the people were put forth, he went in, and took her by the hand, and the maid arose" (Matthew 9:24, 25). Jesus had compassion for this Samaritan woman, and he wanted to perform a miracle to show his love and concern for all humanity. Therefore, He took the opportunity to minister to a sinner, and a distressed soul. Jesus was not critical, biased, nor judgmental to this woman. He established a rapport with her, and got to know her as a person. He did not scale the fish before he caught it, as it is often taught in being an effective witness in ministry.

This woman was not only of a mixed race and an outcast; she was most likely unpopular in her community because of her lifestyle of having five husbands and living with a man. Some of her own people probably cast her out because maybe one of her former husbands was previously another woman's husband, and the man she's with could be somebody else's man. It has been said: "There's nothing worse than a woman's scorn." "You cross her, and she will cross you out." Abram's wife, Sarai, is a prime example of being crossed by her husband's son, Ishmael, when he made fun of her at her husband's sons' feast. Sarai probably said to herself: "I'll fix that." Therefore, she crossed out Hagar and Ishmael, and told her husband that the bondwoman and her son had to go! It is unfortunate that children suffer at the hand of grown folk's business. It was Sarai who initiated the arrangement that her husband sleep with her maid, Hagar, and that he impregnate her: "And Sarai said unto Abram, Behold now, the LORD hath restrained me from bearing: I pray thee, go in unto my maid; it may be that I may obtain children by her. And Abram hearkened to the voice of Sarai" (Genesis 16:2). Ishmael had nothing to do with the arrangements of the three adults. He just took advantage of the opportunity at the feast to throw it in Sarai's face that he was the oldest son of his father, Abram: "And Sarah saw the son of Hagar the Egyptian, which she had born unto Abraham, mocking. Wherefore she said unto Abraham, Cast out this bondwoman and her son: for the son of this bondwoman shall not be heir with my son, even with Isaac" (Genesis 21: 9, 10). Sarah did not care where Hagar and her son, Ishmael went. She just wanted them to be gone and away from her family.

Whereupon, Abraham did not try to negotiate with his wife or communicate with her about where the mother of his child and biological son would have housing or eat; nor did he remind his wife about her initial plan in having him sleep with her maid and impregnate her. Therefore, since Abraham did no such things, he got up early in the morning and took heed to what his wife said in "getting them gone." Prior to them leaving, Abraham did provide them with bread and a bottle of water: "And Abraham rose up early in the morning, and took bread, and a bottle of water, and gave it unto Hagar, putting it on her shoulder, and the child, and sent her away: and she departed, and wandered in the wilderness of Beersheba" (Genesis 21:14).

But God, in His love and mercy, provided for Hagar and her son: "And God heard the voice of the lad; and the angel of God called to Hagar out of heaven, and said unto her, What aileth thee, Hagar? fear not; for God hath heard the voice of the lad where he is" (Genesis 21:17). One can imagine Hagar answering the angel, emotional with tears, saying: "My baby's daddy said his wife told him to tell me that his child and I had to leave their premise, and we are out here all alone. My son is crying now because the water his daddy gave him is all gone, and I don't know where I'm going to get drink and food for him." The situation with Hagar been in the wilderness with her son reminds one of being a single mother, rearing child(ren) along with the absence of the child(ren)'s father. God will take care of them as He did Hagar and Ishmael.

Some people believe that clicks and bullies are only on jobs and in schools; but oh no, these behaviors manifest themselves in some churches and with some church folks. How would you describe Sarah, in her telling her husband what to do about the mother of his child and son, Ishmael?

It appears the Samaritan woman chose to draw water from Jacob's Well when others were not around. If so, could this be to dismiss herself from the emotional distress and gossip of the people in her community?

There were two best friends who reminisced on their previous marriages. The first said: "I was married for over ten years, and I don't know what it feels like to be a wife." The other chimed in with her journey of marriages: "I was married several times, and have yet to have a husband." Another person once said in a humorous and illustrated way, with two sides of a coin: "Some people married, don't want to be married and some people single want to be married." The communications of these people epitomize the downward spiral of the realities in marriages. In the Bible when the people wanted a divorce, the Lord would not grant it at first. Then the people became so adamant about being divorced that God granted Moses to sign the divorce decree: "WHEN a man hath taken a wife, and married her, and it come to pass that she find no favour in his eyes, because he hath found some uncleanness in her: then let him write her a bill of divorcement, and give it in her hand, and send her out of his house" (Deuteronomy 24:1); "He saith unto them, Moses because of the hardness of your hearts suffered you to put away your wives: but from the beginning it was not so" (Matthew 19:8).

A Samaritan Woman

While in theology school, a student (also a pastor in the community) who was very adamant (I do not knock a person's belief) about divorced persons said: "I will not let no person who is divorce be a leader in my church, nor will I ordain them." I realistically responded to the student/pastor: "It's good that your marriage is working out. You never know what life may hold. Life has a way of giving one a curveball, when they are not expected it." Some married people are miserable. They stay in their marriage for several reasons: they hold a certain position in the church or community, their status in life, they hold on to Johnnie Taylor's song *Cheaper To Keep Her*, secretly one (or both) hopes the other will die before them and they will be delivered as a widow or widower, they can play the field in having their cake and eat it too (stay married and have a Boo on the side – When in truth, one needs to adopt the Manhattans song *Let's Just Kiss And Say GoodBye* – Or, do they adopt the other end of the spectrum, and hold on to Al Greens song *Lets Stay Together)*? A man in his mid-60s said: "My wife said we are too old to have sex" (the man was not involved in infidelity. He just did not understand his wife thinking process). The husband was puzzled about this because of their marriage vows, and his wife leadership position in the church, where periodically some of the women in the church would seek her for counsel regarding their marriage.

An evangelist once said in her message: "If women in the church stop giving it up, then ungodly men in the church will have to go elsewhere for their ungodly behavior(s)." The Bible calls ungodly women three things: **silly** "For of this sort are they which creep into houses, and lead captive silly women laden with sins, led away with divers lusts, Ever learning, and never able to come to the knowledge of the truth" (2 Timothy 3:6, 7), **foolish** "A foolish woman is clamorous: she is simple, and knoweth nothing" (Proverbs 9:13), and **strange** "BUT king Solomon loved many strange women, together with the daughter of Pharaoh, women of the Moabites, Ammonites,

Edomites, Zidonians, and Hittites; Of the nations concerning which the LORD said unto the children of Israel, Ye shall not go in to them, neither shall they come in unto you: for surely they will turn away your heart after their gods: Solomon clave unto these in love" (1 Kings 11:1, 2). There may be other unforeseen reasons married people stay in their miserable marriages. Some unhappily married people have sought professional counseling in being a Nicodemus by night (you are in a prestigious position in the church or community, and after the crowd of people; you quietly seek understanding and help from professionals – see John 3:1, 2).

Some people in the community may not have known the history of this Samaritan woman, in her being divorced five times. Maybe, just maybe, this Samaritan woman toiled in her marriages trying to keep it together and her spouses did not work with her, maybe each time she chose the wrong man. On the other hand, maybe this Samaritan woman was in emotionally abusive marriages, where her husbands often told her she was dumb and stupid, and could not do anything right; maybe she was in physically abusive marriages, where her husbands beat her. Could it be, that in the process of time with marriages, this Samaritan woman realized that she is not the married type? Whatever the case may be, this woman decided to get out of her marriages and try living with a man, like so many people (including confessed Christians) do today prior to marriage. They will either live together, or semi-live together; planning a big wedding prior to their marriage. After marriage, she can say like Shug Avery in the *Color Purple* movie: "I'se Married Now!" Believers of Jesus Christ must keep at the forefront that we make plans, but God orders our steps: "The steps of a good man are ordered by the LORD: and he delighteth in his way" (Psalm 37:23). If a person (especially a man), marries too quickly after a divorce or the death of their spouse, some of the saints will say: "They must have been dating," or if he waits too long to remarry, they ask him: "What are you waiting for?"

Several years ago, I was asleep in my bed, and the Lord woke me up in the mid-night hour saying: "I want you to tell her, not to let that man cause her to lose her soul." The Lord did not give me a name for "her." He just put it in my spirit. I told the Lord that He is giving me a hard thing to say. Plus, she lives in another state, I have not seen or talked to her in a very long time. I don't know what's going on with her, and I have never been to her house. After my thinking process, I thought about the prophet Ezekiel, when God told him to tell the people about their sin, and if he did not, the blood was going to be on his hand (Ezekiel 3:18). Therefore, I called her and chatted a few minutes and Afterward said: "You know what? I was sleeping in my bed and the Lord woke me out of my sleep and told me to tell you:" Don't let that man cause you to lose your soul." After hearing the words, the person immediately changed the subject and said "goodbye." The Lord Jesus Christ loves us so much, that He will speak a word for those to tell others far away, and tell others in proximity to each other. There is no distance in the spiritual realm. James Cleveland sings, *Get Right Church*. On the same note, the saints will say: "Get your house in order."

After Jesus established a rapport with the Samaritan woman, he got into her personal life about her husband: "Jesus saith unto her, Go, call thy husband, and come hither" (John 4:16). Sometimes when people want to know if a person is married, they will communicate indirectly, in asking them something about their spouse. In return, the person will unconsciously answer them: "I don't have a spouse," or "he/she plays tennis." Jesus asked this woman to go get her husband, and she plainly told him that she did not have a husband. Afterward, Jesus spoke prophetically to her: "For thou hast had five husbands; and he whom thou now hast is not thy husband: in that saidst thou truly" (verse 18). It was like the prophetic words of Jesus went right over her head, and she started talking about historical things. It did not dawn upon this Samaritan woman who Jesus was, until Jesus reveled himself to her: "Jesus saith unto her, I that speak unto thee am he" (verse 26). This Samaritan woman at Jacob's Well **Decided to Wake Up and Live when she left her waterpot and went into her community to tell the men about The Man, Jesus**: "The woman then left her waterpot, and went her way into the city, and saith to the men, Come, see a man, which told me all things that ever I did: is not this the Christ? Then they went out of the city, and came unto him" (verses 28-30).

The spiritual encounter of Jesus witnessing with the Samaritan woman caused her to forget all about what she came to Jacob's Well to do. Therefore, it is so imperative to ask the Lord how to win souls and love all people with the love of Christ. Sometimes it takes one person to witness to another person, and in return, that person will witness to others. It will become a domino effect; where others become inquisitive about Jesus and their salvation.

After a spiritual encounter with the Lord and salvation, one is not concerned with the naysayers, haters, and gossipers; they have had a personal experience with the Lord, and they must be a witness in their community and abroad. To help keep one from focusing on people hating on them, they can reflect back on Andrae Crouch's song *Take Me* Back. This Samaritan woman went back to the men in her community to witness to them of her spiritual encounter she had with Jesus, and Afterward, the men followed her. This one lady's testimony changed her community in knowing that Jesus knows all about a person, and that He will not cast people out because of their race or lifestyle. He will embrace all with His love and concern for humanity. Moreover, if Believers in their witnessing about salvation and the goodness of Jesus Christ will embrace compassion and love

A Samaritan Woman

in their witnessing, and not be so critical, biased, and judgmental; then just maybe then sinners and former church members will be glad to come into the House of God. Too often some saints of God are ready to scale the fish before they catch it, by preaching denominationalism versus Biblical principles. Also, if more men will follow Godly and redemptive women to the House of God and take their position and responsibilities in affiliating themselves with the Lord and the things of the Lord, then churches will be filled with more men, whom the Lord left in charge as head of their family.

Moral – Biblical and Life-Living:
"JUDGE not, that ye be not judged" (Matthew 7:1)
Some people will throw you under the bus, have no hope for you,
and will put you into hell with no love or compassion –
All because of your race and lifestyle.

Discussion Questions

Do you see any other reason(s) besides Isaac being the heir that caused Sarah to tell her husband, Abraham, that Hagar and her son, Ishmael, had to leave their premise?

What are some ways you can witness to people, when some people consider them an outcast?

Are you open-minded to see how ungodly people can enhance your ministry?

Why are some saints so critical, biased, and judgmental about divorced people, saying they can't get married again because they have a living spouse, they can't be ordained, they can't work in leadership positions in the church, and various reasons?

I Woke Up One Day & Decided to LIVE!

What are some of the ways saints "cast" people out in the Body of Christ?

As a member of the Outreach Ministry, how can you engage others on the team to embrace people like this Samaritan woman?

Why do you believe Jesus went out of His way to be alone with this Samaritan woman?

As a leader in your church, do you see the need for a "Divorce Recovery Ministry" in your local church? If so, who will oversee the ministry, and who will be affiliated with the ministry?

You are ambivalent about filing for a divorce. Is there anybody within the Body of Christ that you can confide in that will give you Godly and wise counsel?

Some people have a great zeal to be on the Outreach Ministry team to witness, but have very little training and skills in witnessing. How can you help them see the need for good training?

Case Studies:
They will not follow the rules of Establishments in the community, and they will often justify their behavior: "I just get happy and feel the spirit of the Lord and pray loud in my prayer with people." The loudness has caused Establishments not to allow this outreach ministry to return. This is the second place of the team's Outreach Ministry of Establishments that they were told: "not to come back."

You are still dealing with the emotional distress from your divorce, with three small children to rear alone. Your ex-spouse has not supported you financially nor does he communicate with his children. You later find out, that one of the sisters in your church is now dating your ex-spouse, and she comes to you for counsel regarding him.

You have been married for 20 years, and the last 15 years has been miserable for you. You two have not slept together, nor had sex in five years. The two of you have sought marriage counseling from a licensed marriage family therapist, and you still feel the same – miserable. You hold a leadership position in the church, and people come to you for counsel. Many have said that you have helped them in many ways.

A sister from the church stops by, and you two are not at home (married couple). Your daughter answers the door and is excited to give her a tour of the house. The tour starts in the living room with her saying in a demonstrative way, with a pat on each couch: "My mother sleeps on this couch, and my daddy sleeps on that couch." The tour continues....

Prayerful Reflection

Dear Father,
Thank You for showing me the importance of realizing how my sins can leave me searching in multiple places with multiple people only to still live life hiding from the judgments of others and dissatisfaction with my life.

Help me not to create Ishmael's in my life, like Sarah. Help me to recognize You and share what You've given me with others so that others can come to know You. Please don't allow me to live hypocritically or judgmentally so that Your light can shine brightly in my life.

Blind Bartimaeus, A Man Who Cried Out for His Deliverance

A Cry of Mercy

"And when he heard that it was Jesus of Nazareth, he began to cry out, and say, Jesus, thou son of David, have mercy on me."
Mark 10:47

The man we call "Blind Bartimaeus," the son of Timaeus, was at the mercy of others to help him maneuver around in life. Jews would have been inquisitive about Bartimaeus' blindness, like Jesus' disciples when they asked: "And his disciples asked him, saying, Master, who did sin, this man, or his parents, that he was born blind" (John 9:2)? Jesus assured them: "Jesus answered, Neither hath this man sinned, nor his parents: but that the works of God should be made manifest in him" (verse 3). The Bible does not give the history of how Bartimaeus became blind. According to the Scripture, we read that he is blind, and that he sits by the highway begging. Was this blind man begging for food, money, prayer, or just a helping hand along the way? Whatever the case may be, he had become invisible to passersby along the way.

Blind Bartimaeus was in the area one day when Jesus and a crowd of people showed up. He was not bothered by the crowd to have his voice heard by Jesus. Prior to Jesus' and the crowd's arrival, Blind Bartimaeus would have sat alone, trying to get a helping hand, begging from passersby along the way. Imagine that he began looking with hope to his future and to prosperity. With this gleam of faith, he would not continue to focus on his disability. One can imagine a person in his condition reflecting on the late Rev. Timothy Wright's song, *It Won't Be This Way Always.* It is an assurance that the people of God must cry out for their deliverance like this blind man, Bartimaeus. A song can bring comfort and hope to soothe the heavy burden.

Time after time, Blind Bartimaeus was at the mercy of others to lead him along the way, even to the corner to beg. He finally got tired of his condition, and when he knew Jesus was near, he made a judgment call to step out in faith and believe that the Lord Jesus Christ would deliver him and make him whole. The opportunity presented itself, one particular day when Blind Bartimaeus heard that Jesus was in the area, and when he heard the footsteps and cries of many; he knew that some way, somehow or another, through the crowds of people, he had to be heard, seen, and ultimately healed by Jesus. A blind person will look for other faculties of their body to help them maneuver in life. Blind Bartimaeus used his ears. He knew the people would pay him no mind, so he took matters into his own hands. He likely thought back on the children of Israel who "cried out to the God of Abraham, the God of Isaac, and the God of Jacob." This blind man cried out: "Jesus, thou son of David, have mercy on me" (Mark 10:47b). In the midst of a great number of people, Blind Bartimaeus made sure that he would not miss his opportunity to be heard by Jesus; so he cried out with words that got people's attention. Some people tried to hush the blind man, but the Bible says that he cried out the more: "Thou son of David, have mercy on me" (verse 48b).

Blind Bartimaeus was tired and at his wit's end with needing the service of others. He could not keep quiet, and the people could not hush the cry of this man. This cry was so vibrant that: "Jesus stood still, and commanded him to be called" (verse 49a). The disciples

Blind Bartimaeus, A Man Who Cried Out for His Deliverance

had to respond to the command of Jesus and told Blind Bartimaeus: "rise; he calleth thee" (verse 49b). In the Old Testament, the Lord commanded blessings for obedience: "The LORD shall command the blessing upon thee in thy storehouses, and in all that thou settest thine hand unto; and he shall bless thee in the land which the LORD thy God giveth thee" (Deuteronomy 28:8); for the prophet Elijah to be fed by ravens and for a widow to sustain him: "I have commanded the ravens to feed thee there" (I Kings 17:4b); "I have commanded a widow woman there to sustain thee" (verse 9b). The command of the Lord also went forth for Blind Bartimaeus to come to Jesus. The Lord will command the least likely people and circumstances in order to bless His people.

God has commanded His people to bless others also. Several years ago, I woke up one morning and looked in my refrigerator and cabinets and said to myself: "Ain't no food in there for me and my kids. I'll just go to Sunday School and then I'll worry about that later." I was a new member at this particular church and didn't know many people there. After the closing of Sunday School, I went to the sanctuary and sat in the congregation prior to Sunday morning service getting started. As I sat there, this sister walked up to me and dropped some money in my lap saying: "The Lord told me to give this to you." I responded: "I can't take your money" (knowing all along I needed it). She said exuberantly, with both hands lifted up: "I can't take it back, you can't pay me back, nor can you give it back to me. I have to do just what the Lord told me to do!" At that moment, I wanted to jump up and run all around the church thanking God for commanding this sister to bless me with grocery money. The Lord gave a command to this sister, and she responded. After church, I went to the grocery store. The following Sunday, I told her my testimony about not having grocery money (which was an embarrassment to me), how she obeyed the Lord to bless me, and that she had not moved on her own accord. It was a "Thus saith the Lord" move!

Years passed, and I was in another state when the Lord spoke to me saying: "Send Gail a hundred dollars." I responded to the Lord: "I'm hurting too" (I had money in the bank for an emergency). The Lord spoke the same words to me: "Send Gail a hundred dollars." I responded: "Lord, I don't know what's going on with her. I haven't talked to Gail in years." Later, the Lord put those words of "Send Gail . . ." in my spirit and wouldn't let it go. Finally, I said: "Lord, I better do what you said or else you're going to get me." I obeyed the Lord, and mailed one hundred dollars to her. Upon receiving the money, Gail called me and thanked me with this testimony: "Me and my husband were here (another state), and we didn't have no food; so we prayed to the Lord, and you sent us a hundred dollars from another state." There is no distance in the spiritual realm when the people of God pray and cry out to Him.

It is ironic that at times some people, who are walking with the leader and trying to get their own deliverance from the Lord will have the audacity to try to hold another person back from their own deliverance - trying to hush them and saying: "It don't take all that." If it wasn't for the Lord, where would Blind Bartimaeus be? The Lord made a difference in this blind man's life. Blind Bartimaeus was not about to miss his blessing. He had been at the mercy of people too long, and he knew he had to cry out for his deliverance. God honored his hope and his faith.

When Jesus called Blind Bartimaeus, he rose up and came to Jesus. This blind man and beggar did not ask for help! He made his own way to Jesus, through the people-blindness, poverty and all: "And he, casting away his garment, rose, and came to Jesus" (Mark 10:50). Blind Bartimaeus was determined to receive his eyesight and to get out of poverty and being in need of folks. Jesus had made the command that he be called. Jesus did not act like the other people walking along the road, seeing but ignoring the blind man in need. Jesus saw him and asked him a question: "What wilt thou that I should do unto thee" (Mark 10:51a)? Blind Bartimaeus did not relate his history like King Solomon, when God asked him a similar question: "Ask what I shall give thee" (1 Kings 3:5b). King Solomon reminisced about his father, David, who had it in his heart to build God a house, him being a child with adult responsibilities, and making decisions over God's people, etc. Blind Bartimaeus got right to his need. He jumped in with both feet and told the Lord what his cry represented: "Lord, that I might receive my sight" (Mark 10:51b). Blind Bartimaeus' faith to be healed and his cry for mercy brought deliverance, and he immediately received his sight.

The crowd had seen Blind Bartimaeus rise up, when he came to Jesus to receive his eyesight. Oh, the people tried to hush the blind man and cut off his blessing, but this man was determined to overcome his troubles. The blessings of God are there to be received and not "cut off." Miami Mass Choir sings: *It Is For Me.* The Lord had a blessing for this blind man. It started with a cry for mercy, and it ended with his faith to be made whole. **Blind Bartimaeus Woke Up and Decided to Live when he considered a life of waiting for people to guide him around, and being at the mercy of others as he sat on the road begging for a helping hand.** This "One Day" of waking up with a cry of mercy ended up being Bartimaeus' day of deliverance.

Moral – Biblical and Life-Living:
Keep sitting and waiting on folks, and you'll be up a creek without a paddle.

I Woke Up One Day & Decided to LIVE!

Discussion Questions

Do you see some associations between Blind Bartimaeus and people today standing on the street corner asking for a "helping hand?" If so, what are they?

Some people will leech off people and suck them dry, without being a helping hand to others. What are some ways to help these people be independent and to give back to others?

At what point in one's life do they get tired of waiting on folks, until it causes them to cry out for "mercy?"

Has the Lord ever commanded you to bless someone? If so, did you immediately respond or did you try to rationalize it and ignore the command to bless.

Case Study:
You are in true need of being delivered from poverty. You are a faithful tithe payer, and your offering envelope contains half of your tithes. While at the same time, poverty tends to linger with you. You seek the Lord for an answer, and He commands you this week to bless someone in your church with your last $200.00.

Blind Bartimaeus, A Man Who Cried Out for His Deliverance

Prayerful Reflection

Dear Father,
Thank You for helping me to understand the importance of not worrying about the responses of others when I am in desperate need. Help me to humble myself and trust in Your love and merciful kindness. May I be willing to cry out to You knowing that You will hear me.

Teach me, Lord, to respond to Your instructions when You want to use me to be a blessing to others. Help me not to respond selfishly, but to remember that everything I have I have only because You have provided it. As I cry out to You may others hear and see You respond so they can learn of Your goodness too.

Life-Living Perspective

Home Run with a Curve Ball

Some church folks don't want to talk about life-living situations, because "you're saved, sanctified, Holy Ghost-filled, and going on with Jesus." Plus, some life-living situations can be "hush and taboo" in the Body of Christ. Therefore, since some Believers in the Body of Christ do not want to talk about life-living situations, the Lord has raised up people who will. The Lord will never be without a witness: "Nevertheless he left not himself without witness, in that he did good, and gave us rain from heaven, and fruitful seasons, filling our hearts with food and gladness" (Acts 14:17). Mr. Tyler Perry, Bishop T.D. Jakes, the late Bishop Eddie Long, and others present the "hush and taboo" in plays, movies, and published books. Churches and ministries who choose not to talk about them often end up paying money to see those who choose to talk about the "hush and taboo." They are going to their plays, buying their books, having small group discussions, facilitating their books in weekly Bible study, and looking at them on television and laughing with them; while prior to this, they were "hush and taboo" in the Body of Christ.

A professional baseball pitcher will not always throw a "straight pitch" to the batter. He or she will throw a fast curveball that will at times throw the batter for a loop. The curveball can be a spin, fast or slow ball, an under or over throw, or one that comes out of nowhere. In the movie, *A Soldier's Story*, CJ was an awesome baseball player that had a few curve balls thrown at him as a "batter." In one scene, he swung a few strikes before striking out. He told the pitcher to send another throw. The pitcher threw a curve ball to CJ who hit a home run with a burst of shouts from many in the crowd. In truth, life-living itself will give one a curveball that will cause a few "strikeouts." Sometimes, people will go down the same road looking for different results, but the results will be the same and sometimes worse. A person on the outside looking in will ask: "Haven't you learned your lesson?" The person's response may be: "You just don't have a point of reference," or "You just don't understand the situation." My mother has said to some of her seven children: "When you hit it, you'll know." In other words, "when reality sets in, you'll wake up and really see the situation(s) you keep putting yourself in."

People talk about prisoners being in a revolving door when getting out of prison and then going back in for the same thing(s) or even for a new charge(s). Some people who have never been incarcerated tend to portray this same type of behavior in other ways: relationships (marrying the same kind of person), quitting jobs without another job at hand, and getting out of debt yet before the year is over - back in debt, rationalizing when the Lord has said differently, etc. When one cannot decide, they are often told: "You are wishy-washy." Could it be a childhood pattern that tends to resurface, and the person is unconsciously falling into old patterns?

Throughout the Bible, we read about Biblical persons who received God's blessing based upon their obedience. Abraham is a prime example of one obeying God and being blessed: "And I will make thy seed to multiply as the stars of heaven, and will give unto thy seed all these countries; and in thy seed shall all the nations of the earth be blessed; Because that Abraham obeyed my voice, and kept my charge, my commandments, my statutes, and my laws" (Geneses 26:4, 5). For some reason or another, some have not continued to follow the example of Abraham's obedience to God. Therefore, this has caused them to fall into the enemy's trap, where their weakness took its toil. Life-living situations threw a curve ball at them, and they chose not to take another swing with a curveball after striking out. Others choose to be more prepared for a curveball in their life, and therefore live more vibrantly.

Moral – Biblical and Life-Living:
Life is fickle, and you never know when it'll give you a curve ball.

Discussions Questions

Why do some Believers of Jesus Christ keep going down the same road with bad decisions, while looking for a better or different outcome?

Let's take a moment to look at "leaders" in the church who choose not to talk about "real life-living situations." What are some areas that tend to be "hush and taboo" in the church?

Case Study:
Associate Pastor Jonah Sweet and his wife, Susan, had sought marriage counseling from their pastor, John Letton, who has very little experience in couple counseling. (NOTE: As a pastor, counseling and pastoral duties go hand-in-hand). Sister Sweet believes that the Lord has called her as a minister, and her husband believes differently. In their counseling session, she tells the pastor about her love for Jesus Christ, her calling as a minister, and her desire to be on the ministerial staff. In return the pastor tells her with a stern look on his face: "Your home ain't right." She looks at him with disbelief, saying to herself: "I can't believe he is ministering in partiality, where I see judgment and bias." She comes to herself and responds to him with a question and concern: "How about him; he's in the marriage too, and you let him go forth as a minister?" The

pastor assures her: "Oh, he's just working in that position." She looks at him with a spirit of humanity, and at the same time, speaks her mind: "Yea, right!" Sister Sweet walks out of the session, with that one tear slowly running down her face, and the second tear catches up.

Prayerful Reflection

Dear Father,
Thank You for being there when life throws me curveballs. With Your help, I'll come to recognize the patterns that keep me from experiencing victory. Eventually I'll learn from my mistakes and be an example to others that they should keep trying til they hit it a homerun, even when life throws them a curveball.

Final Prayerful Reflection

Dear Father,
Thank You for giving me an opportunity to read this book and reflect upon the reality that every time my life encounters difficulty that brings me to the point of despair, I have an opportunity to make a choice to speak, think, and behave in ways that bring life or death.

With each example given I could see chapters from my life, the lives of those I love, and the lives of others I've encountered. I realize more than ever before that You really have laid a foundation for me to LIVE!

Help me not to be distracted by the things other people do or don't do, say or don't say, nor the circumstances that seem insurmountable. Cause me to recognize that Your presence with me, if I choose to acknowledge it, has the power to change my perspective and outcome for the better.

Thank You for the Biblical accounts that leave a blueprint for me to follow. May I avoid the discontent of the Israelites in the wilderness, and the lustful desires of Sampson. May I remember to encourage myself as I reflect upon the faith I have in Your willingness and ability to help me.

May the reality that sitting in the midst of hopeless moments waiting for the end, is fruitless cause me to get up and at least make an effort to live. May I overcome moments of despair in order to be a guide to others whose desire is to go even farther than I will.

As I share the truths You share with me in our times together yield a testimony that have the power to bring whole cities to You. May Your children cry out to You in unity so that the world can see how much You love us all.

I Woke Up One Day & Decided to LIVE!

Last but not least, Father, when life throws us curveballs, may we hit the ball of life out of the park causing the hearts of those around us to stand to their feet in amazement at the wonder and glory of Your love. In the matchless name of Your Son, Jesus, Amen.

References

American Psychiatric Association (2013). *Diagnostic and statistical manual of mental disorders, fifth edition* (DSM-5). Arlington, VA: Author.

Baldwin, J. (1963). The fire next time. New York: The Dial Press.

Bitter, J. (2009). Theory and practice of family therapy and counseling. Belmont,CA Brooks/Cole, Cengage Learning.

Douglass, F. (1986). *Narrative of the life of Frederick Douglass, An american slave*. New York: Penguin Books.

Dunbar, Paul (1993). *We wear the mask*, edited by Joanne M. Braxton, pp.71. Charlottesville & London: The University Press of Virginia.

Frangipane, F. (1991). *The Jezebel spirit*. Cedar Rapids, IA: Arrow Publications.

Hughes, L. (1961). The best of Simple. New York: Noonday Press.

Long, Eddie (1999). I don't want Delilah, I need you! (what a woman needs to know – what a man needs to understand). New York: Albury Publishing.

Martin, M. (2002). Saving our last nerve: The Black woman's path to mental health. Roscoe, IL: Hilton Publishing Company.

Mays, B, (1971). *Born to rebel: An autobiography*. The University of Georgia Press: Athens, Georgia.

Mays, B. (1969). *Disturbed about man*. Virginia: John Knox Press.

McGee, V. (1982). Thru the Bible, Vol II. Tennessee: Thomas Nelson Publishers.

Morpurgo, M. (2004). *Aesop's* fables. London: Orchard Books.

NAMI: National Alliance on Mental Illness/Understanding Health Insurance. Internet: https://www.nami.org.

Walker, Margaret Retrieved *The Color Purple*. Internet: www.alchetron.com.

Walsh, F. (2016). *Strengthening family resilience* (3rd ed.). New York: Guilford Press.

Williams, D. (2002). The Jezebel spirit: Freeing yourself from the spirit of control. United States: Decapolis Publishing.

Retrieved January 10, 2010 (https://en.wikipedia.org/wiki/The_Talented_Tenth).

Retrieved January 10, 2010 (https://en.wikipedia..org/wiki/Social_change).

Retrieved January 12, 2010 (http://www.bible.ca/... god-strikes-sinners-with-insanty.htm

About the Author

Carron Caldwell holds a Master's degree from Grand Rapids Theological Seminary (Grand Rapids, MI) in counseling ministry. She has a master's degree from Cornerstone University (Grand Rapids, MI) in ministry leadership. Carron also has a specialization in Couple and Family Counseling from Oakland University (Rochester, MI). She holds a Master's degree in Christian education from Emmanuel Theological Seminary (Nashville, TN), a Bachelor of Theology degree in church vocations from American Baptist College (Nashville, TN), a bachelor degree in history from Tennessee State University (Nashville, TN), and an associate degree in general studies from Highland Park Community College (Highland Park, MI). She is a licensed professional counselor (LPC), and a supervisor to limited licensed professional counselors (LLPC). Carron Caldwell has a heart for outreach ministry, and she believes that churches that can and will, should have a full-time paid "Director of Ministry" in their local church to oversee ministries.

www.ingramcontent.com/pod-product-compliance
Lightning Source LLC
Chambersburg PA
CBHW052145110526
44591CB00012B/1867